# Koi Crazy

written by Peter M. Waddington

~~~~~~~~~~~~~~~~~~~~~~~~~~~~~~~~~~~~~~~~~~~~~~~~~~~~~~~~~~~~~~~~~~

First published in 2009 by Peter Waddington.

Copyright Peter Waddington 2009.

Illustrations by Satoru Hoshino 1988 and Geoff Nuttall 2008.

Photographs by Peter Waddington, Jasper Kujiper, Peter Chester and Stewart Jones.
~~~~~~~~~~~~~~~~~~~~~~~~~~~~~~~~~~~~~~~~~~~~~~~~~~~~~~~~~~~~~~~~~~

All rights reserved. No part of this book may be reproduced into a retrieval system, nor may it be transmitted in any form or by any means (electronic, mechanical, photocopying, recording or otherwise) without the signed and written permission of Peter Waddington.

The right of Peter Waddington to be identified as author has been asserted to him in accordance with the Copyright, Designs and Patent Act 1988.

**ISBN…….. 978-0-9526381-2-4**

British Library Cataloguing-in-Publication Data.

A catalogue record is available for this book from the British Library.

Layout by Peter Waddington and Stewart Jones.

Printed by Copytech (UK) Ltd., 9, Culley Court, Bakewell Road, Orton, Southgate, Peterborough PE2 6XD.

# 'KOI CRAZY'
## Modern-day Koi keeping for everyone
### Written by Peter Waddington

MY AIMS :–

'This book is intended to assist both the many enthusiastic apprentices as well as the more experienced enthusiasts in the hobby of Koi keeping who may, from time to time, find themselves confused with some certain areas of the total subject.

The book covers ALL the many and varied aspects of keeping Koi and also highlights pitfalls and costly mistakes to avoid. As a result this should then enable the reader to enjoy this truly fascinating hobby to the full.'

## About the author

Peter Waddington saw his first Koi in 1972 and opened the first 'Koi-only dealership' anywhere outside of Japan in 1979.

He has since supplied 17 out of 25 'Supreme Champion Koi' to the UK 'BKKS National' Koi shows held since 1982 and to many other major Koi shows all around the world where they have also taken the highly coveted 'Supreme Champion' award.

His first visit to Japan was in 1977 and countless trips to purchase stocks and to to learn more have followed over the years. He estimates that, if the duration of all his visits were added together, he would have spent, by now, over seven years actually living in the major Koi producing areas of Japan. He also has no hesitation in freely admitting that over 85% of the knowledge that he has amassed over the years, regarding Koi, Koi appreciation, Koi pond design and modern methods of Koi pond filtration has been learned from the Japanese breeders themselves where he is widely known by all simply as 'Mr. Peter'.

He published his first book 'Koi Kichi' in 1995 which was met with world-wide acclaim. His second, far more lavish book, was published in late 2004 entitled 'Koi2Kichi' where sales to date have equalled his expectations.

He has also designed and installed many purpose-made Koi pond and filter systems for enthusiasts all over the world since 1979.

You can find more detailed information on Peter and a greater insight into the worldwide hobby of keeping Koi by visiting his website www.koikichi.com

The author's own Koi pond completed in 1999

# Contents

**1. 'Preface'** – (pages 1-6) An introduction to the hobby of keeping Koi

**2. 'History'** – (pages 7-10) The true origins of Koi

**3. 'Nishikigoi'** – (pages 11-22) Varieties, Pattern-styles & show classifications

**4. 'Pond'** – (pages 23-32) Koi pond design & construction methods

**5. 'Filter'** – (pages 33-50) Understanding filtration, filter designs, related items

**6. 'Temperature'** – (pages 51-52) The advantages of using heat economically

**7. 'Water'** - (pages 53-56) Maturing & maintaining pond water requirements

**8. 'Feeding'** – (pages 57-58) Throughout the year

**9. 'Caring'** – (pages 59-66) Parasitic & bacterial disorders, detection, treatment

**10. 'Miscellany'** – (pages 67-74) Handling, Breeding, Salinity; Showing, Quarantine etc.

**11. 'My Mentors'** – (pages 75-89) In praise of those who produce Nishikigoi

# 1. PREFACE

This book was initially written, and intended for, those who are novices or potential newcomers to the fascinating hobby of keeping Koi and is produced to explain all the major facets of the hobby in detail. I have used some pictures, illustrations and texts etc. from my previous books as they are just as accurate and as valid today – as always, don't fix it - if it's not broken.

However, this same book is as 'up-to-the-minute' as is possible today in 2009 whereby no important corners have been cut and no important texts have been omitted. As a result the detailed information in this book should be very useful to all Koi enthusiasts irrespective of the actual length of time they have experience of the hobby.

I have attempted to write this book in a 'straight-talking, direct and factual style' and without the inclusion of the distracting and unecessary 'arty' graphics of today which I detest and, for me, only serve as 'padding'. Furthermore I am sure that the book does not 'talk down' to the reader in any way. I sincerely hope it will assist the reader to reject the many pitfalls given by wrong or bad advice, superstition, exaggeration or simple ignorance. This should then allow enthusiasts to avoid making costly mistakes in purchasing inferior or unsuitable equipment and other items that are not really up to the job in hand.

Koi are truly beautiful creatures and the hobby of keeping them grows with each passing year. This can be witnessed by the increasing number of retail outlets selling Koi today which have been imported from many countries around the world.

Today there are avid Koi enthusiasts from all over the globe. Many of whom started out with an innocent visit to a garden centre which initially sparked their enthusiasm after seeing their very first Koi in the flesh before them.

I started keeping Koi back in 1972 when the hobby was in its infancy in the UK. Since 1978, I have been involved with Koi and all the related keeping techniques, on a day to day basis, as a full-time occupation.

I can assure the reader that I have made **ALL** the mistakes there are to make many times over and have learned, to my significant costs in both labour and money, the error of my ways.

- **If I had been able to obtain and read this very same book in 1972 it would have saved me many thousands of pounds and months of mis-spent labours.**

Today's garden pond market is significant and thousands of newcomers come into the picture every spring when they visit a local garden centre and decide they will purchase the necessary items for their own garden to build a pond in which to house pet fish.

The actual desire to keep Koi in their pond usually comes about later and soon it will become very evident that a simple garden pond, despite how aesthetically pleasing, is not a suitable home for these creatures.

They are then faced with hundreds of products which vary from outlet to outlet. They are next given much conflicting advice which also varies greatly from outlet to outlet, as well as from various other sources. Is it little wonder that the vast majority of new garden ponds installed each year become total disasters after only a few short months of completion?

More often than not, these 'disasters' are eventually broken down, removed and then re-instated to become flower beds once more.

*In view of the above I would strongly advise the newcomer to discount ANY and ALL information he/she has been given about this subject in advance and, instead, start a new learning curve here with a totally blank and fresh mind.*

Before I continue further and despite what many still profess, there is nothing at all **'natural'** about our garden Koi ponds even if they are home to water plants, lilies, rocks, streams and waterfalls etc.

Please do remember that only 'nature' produces natural ponds - and these evolve over decades – totally unlike garden Koi ponds which require both manual excavation and waterproofing.

*The initial task of putting the first spade in the ground should settle, for once and for all, that this is not, in any way, 'natural'.*

**Low stocking rates of Koi thriving in the green water of a natural, unfiltered private lake**

Instead, our garden Koi ponds should really be 'garden aquariums' which, like all good aquariums, desperately need filtration systems. We should also provide and install simple and easy methods of removing the waste which is being produced constantly with each passing hour in our Koi ponds.

Despite what we are continually told elsewhere, it is totally impossible for us humans to strike a 'natural balance' as found in nature, with our own garden Koi pond.

Instead we attempt, by 'man-made, modern technology', to simulate those conditions found in nature in order to provide an environment for our Koi to **thrive** in perfect health, and not just merely 'survive'. As we all know, there is a vast difference between the words 'survive' and 'thrive'.

Koi are nowhere near as hardy as other species of domestic garden pond fish and so we need to give them much more consideration in our keeping techniques.

Those amongst us who still persevere in building a simple waterproof 'hole in the ground' and then filling it with water will soon realise that, by adding fish, plants, food and more food, the 'pond' is little more than a man-made cesspit. Some even advocate placing rocks, pebbles and gravel on the base of the pond! This requires regular emptying plus laborious cleaning and re-filling which is necessary and vital if the fish are to survive. It then becomes more like constant hard labour rather than the enjoyable pastime it should be!

This type of pond may well be acceptable as a bog garden for plants, frogs and newts etc. but it is completely useless for keeping fish life of ANY kind.

**This is a typical, partially-drained, Japanese mud pond used only from June to October for growing Koi during the warm summer months at very low stocking rates. These ponds are excavated by huge machines and the clay base and sides are also compressed by machine.**

None of these ponds are 'natural' in any way and have no new water entering or exiting them. When these ponds are harvested during October, all the water is drained away by siphon or drains. After this, any waste debris is removed and the bases and sides are compressed by machine once again.

Once the keeper realises the above there is then another quandary as to the type of filter and other equipment needed – hopefully this book will clarify all of these matters.

Badly-designed garden Koi ponds and ignorance are generally the causes of the huge pet fish losses which are commonplace all over the world, whereas experienced Koi keepers rarely lose Koi. Hopefully this book will help prevent some more of these losses.

Keeping Koi properly can sometimes be an expensive hobby depending on how far you wish to get into it but 'keeping Koi badly' alas, will always remain a very expensive pastime indeed!

The ponds and filtration systems outlined in this book should provide an ideal home for all types of pond fish although they are specifically designed with Koi in mind. In short, they are true 'no-nonsense' Koi ponds.

Also the filtration systems detailed are designed and employed to cope easily with the volume of water within the total system. This means that a larger pond thus necessitates a larger filter system than one that is required for a smaller pond.

### Ready-made filter system

Furthermore all the filter systems described in this book require periodic maintenance to flush away unwanted faeces and build-up of other waste matter.

Do remember, no system, irrespective of how 'state-of-the-art' it may be, is ever 'maintenance-free'.

- Please note - A simple example and calculation of a filter being powered by a pump delivering only a modest 500 gallons per hour means that the filter has to be capable of processing 12,000 gallons of water and associated debris each day - or a very sobering 4,380,000 gallons per year!

In view of this, the filter must be efficient enough to handle this significant volume of water.

Thankfully and in truth, **'pure simplicity and common sense'** are the real keys to designing a perfect garden pond and filtration system for your Koi as will be shown later in this book.

Do make sure that all items of equipment and valves incorporated are easy to access for periodic maintenance otherwise this can become a real chore. As to the quality of equipment purchased please remember that these items are generally in operation permanently and it is rare indeed that 'the cheapest is the best'.

The single and most important aspect of successful Koi keeping is the design, build and running operation of the overall pond system which will give a healthy and permanent home to your pets. The correct design, installation and operation of a system provides a vital and valuable tool in the overall hobby of keeping Koi.

The importance of this cannot be overstated – in view of this it is essential that the correct system is installed and no compromises are made nor any corners cut. As mentioned earlier, Koi are truly beautiful creatures and it is our duty as Koi keepers to look after them properly.

**Adult Koi at feeding time**

**One year old Koi at feeding time**

To those readers who have already built a system, hopefully this book may assist in making some improvements in certain areas.

To others planning a new system, once again, it is recommended that this book is thoroughly read and understood before finalising any plans already made.

Also, if this book leaves the reader seeking more and more information, there are many Koi Societies in most parts of the world that one can join. There are various Koi websites where one can get information from some very experienced enthusiasts. There are also several specialist Koi magazines, both monthly and quarterly, available by subscription.

Koi keepers come from all walks of life and many different backgrounds, they are also at various stages of the hobby. There is no definite period of time for 'apprenticeship' in this hobby as sheer enthusiasm generally makes for rapid learning and this is true in any given subject.

Once again, the contents of this book cover all the most important aspects of Koi keeping but there are many more skills one can learn once these basics have been thoroughly digested. Keeping Koi should be an enjoyable, fulfilling and relaxing hobby, hopefully this book should assist everyone reading it in making it just that.

Wishing you all success in this fascinating hobby of ours.

Peter Waddington 2009

This truly magnificent Kohaku on the left is the current UK 'BKKS National Show Champion in 2008' - she also took the very same award in 2007.

I sourced this Koi from Toshio Sakai in Isawa and she is owned by Bill Oakley from the Midlands.

To retain this totally perfect body shape at almost 90cms is not an easy task. To find Koi of this rare quality anywhere in the world today is almost impossible – even if money proves to be of no object.

PS. If you are unsure of **any** aspects covered in the text of this book you can email me at koi2kichi@aol.com for further clarification.

# 2. HISTORY

The correct name today for 'Koi Carp' as many generally refer to them is 'NISHIKIGOI' *(nish-key-goy)* – taken from the Japanese term which translates as 'brocaded carp'. The Japanese words 'Koi' or 'Goi' simply translate as 'Carp'. The real origin of these creatures was, in truth, more of an accident than by any real intentions and they are truly 'man-made' - albeit originating from the ancient, wild black carp known in Japan as 'Magoi'.

**Japanese-bred Magoi 99cms. – this is in the owner's pond and weighed 50 pounds (22kg) in 2003!**

Magoi – *(Latin name 'Cyprinus Carpio')* were originally only indigenous to the temperate climate areas surrounding the Caspian Sea and were, in later years, introduced to many other parts of the world for valuable food purposes via the Crusaders and the monks.

During the middle part of the 19th. Century, Magoi were imported from China into Japan to be bred as a food fish. Some were introduced into a mountainous area in Niigata Prefecture then known as 'Nijimura' which later became called 'Yamakoshi' as it is still known today. Yamakoshi is, and always has been, the world centre of Nishikigoi production with some 400 breeders based in the surrounding mountainside villages.

**Yamakoshi spring scene showing mud ponds *('doro-ike')* being filled again after the winter snows. Koi will be introduced to these ponds in mid-June. The large hoses shown are used for transferring water by siphon from higher ponds to those lower down the mountainsides.**

**Yamakoshi winter scenes showing mud ponds filled with snow water**

This area in winter can have snowfalls of 5 metres deep coupled with summers of intense heat. The original plan was to breed the Magoi males and females in spring and grow the fry throughout the summer months in the warm water reservoirs high in the mountains which were used to irrigate the rice paddies that were excavated lower down the mountainsides.

By mid October the fry were around 4" (10cms) long and could be harvested, salted and stored for food. These young carp could then be eaten during the harsh winter period ahead when most villagers were housebound due to the heavy snowfalls and at a time when supplies of animal protein were almost impossible to find.

Parent carp were usually kept indoors for winter in 'ponds' dug into the floors of dwelling houses. They had to be kept there during the winter to protect them against the freezing outdoor temperatures until they could be used to spawn and produce fry again during the following spring.

The parent carp originated from different strains of Magoi initially imported from several lines *('Tetsu Magoi' and 'Asagi Magoi' being the most prominent)* yet all these Magoi produced fry which made valuable edible food for the table.

During some harvests of the small Magoi it was noted that a few showed the odd, coloured scale, presumably due to interbreeding of these different strains of parent Magoi. Some carp farmers kept these as their own pets and, purely as a private hobby, bred them with other carp from local farmers that were also showing some coloured scales.

At around the turn of the Century there were several small breeders producing 'coloured carp' *(then known as 'Irogoi')* purely for ornamental purposes. They were also selling some of their production to wealthy professional people in the surrounding areas who had ornamental garden ponds in which to keep them. In those times it was only possible to transport them for short distances.

- In 1914 the Tokyo Taisho Exhibition was held and 28 Irogoi, from Yamakoshi, were transported by slow train in badly-leaking wooden ponds and displayed to the Japanese public for the very first time. Many were lost in transportation and also during the exhibition itself. The surviving Koi were then taken from the exhibition afterwards and introduced into the huge moat which surrounded the Emperor's castle in the centre of Tokyo.

- Most Koi and parent Koi were lost in the mountains during the second world war and serious attempts in breeding could only be continued in earnest after the war ended.

- However it was not until the early 1960's that Nishikigoi really became well known to the other parts of Japan and this was directly after the invention of the vinyl bag. It was soon learned that the bag could be filled with water and then inflated with pure oxygen for safe transportation of the Koi – hitherto this was not possible.

- During the mid-1960's Nishikigoi became very popular in Japan and have since been exported to many countries all over the world.

- The first Nishikigoi were imported into the UK during 1966 and, soon afterwards, a few enthusiasts began to collect them and then form Societies and clubs in order to further their knowledge on basic Koi keeping methods.

- In 1969 the first Koi show was held in Japan.

- The British Koi Keepers Society was formed in 1970 and is still going strong today.

- In 1975, the first Koi show ever held outside of Japan was in my own back garden.

**Modern day Koi show in Japan**

Japan still produces the finest quality Koi available today by far, and this is why Japanese-bred Koi continue to command the highest prices in the world market.

There are many Nishikigoi shows held in various parts of Japan today, the most important are as follows:-

- The 'All-Japan' show held in late January in Tokyo. This is staged by the All-Japan Dealer's Association (Shinkokai).

- The Zen Nippon Airinkai show (a large, amateur organisation) held annually in various parts of Japan during November.

- The Wakaigoi (young Koi) show staged annually in April in Ojiya City.

- The No-gyo-sai (agricultural show) staged annually in Ojiya City in late October.

### 'Doris'

This very famous Sanke is known by many simply as 'Doris'. She is, by far, the finest Nishikigoi that has ever passed through my hands in some 26 years of scouring Japan to find very rare specimens.

***She may also be the very best Koi I have ever seen with my own two eyes – and, believe me, I have seen a few!***

She holds the incredible record of receiving three 'Supreme Champion' awards at the BKKS 'National' shows in 1997, 1998 and 2000. I cannot see her record ever being beaten or even equalised in the near future.

Doris was bought by Bill Oakley in the UK and this picture was taken when she was nine years old and 90cms. She is from true 'Matsunosuke Magoi Bloodline' and was bred by Toshio Sakai of the Isawa Nishikigoi Center in Yamanashi.

**Doris is, without doubt, my greatest single achievement in Nishikigoi.**

As the quality of production gets better with each passing year in other countries so does the quality of Japanese production where some 700 Koi breeders compete against each other for a share of the home and export market.

### Selecting Nishikigoi at the Yagenji Koi farm in Mushigame village.

Nowadays Koi are bred in countries other than Japan such as Israel; Singapore; USA; UK; South East Asia and China. Generally these Koi are substantially cheaper than Japanese Koi and also provide an excellent cost alternative for those just starting out in the hobby.

As to the subjects of size and longevity, the largest Nishikigoi that I have ever seen measured 1 metre and 40cms and the oldest I know of is 34 years. There are only a handful of Koi that have ever exceeded 1 metre and the average lifespan is around 25 years.

# 3. NISHIKIGOI VARIETIES

## (PLUS PATTERN STYLES & SHOW CLASSIFICATIONS)

Over the years there have been many different varieties of Nishikigoi produced which have led to an assortment of show classifications, colours and pattern styles. The following unique paintings are taken from my first book entitled 'Koi Kichi' *(The Japanese term for 'Koi Crazy')* first published in 1995. These paintings are still a **very unique and accurate coverage** of most of the varieties one can see for sale today although several examples are becoming quite rare and increasingly hard to find.

To obtain actual photographs of all these varieties is almost impossible – location, size, sex and 'posing' all produce very real problems. These paintings below were commissioned by myself in 1988 and were hand-painted on a standard female Koi outline prepared by Nishikigoi artist Satoru Hoshino of Oyiya City who is also a famous local Nishikigoi historian.

### Show Classifications

*(Inverted commas denote classification rather than variety)*

1. Kohaku
2. Sanke
3. Showa
4. Tancho
5. Bekko
6. 'Utsurimono'
7. 'Koromo'
8. Kin/Gin Rin
9. Asagi/Shusui
10. 'Hikarimuji'
11. 'Hikarimoyo'
12. 'Hikariutsuri'
13. 'Kawarimono'
14. Doitsu

### UK Size Classifications

*(All Koi are sized by the benching teams on entry to the show.)*

- Size One – up to 25cm
- Size Two – up to 35cms
- Size Three – up to 45cms
- Size Four – up to 55cms
- Size Five – up to 65cms
- Size Six – up to 75cms
- Size Seven – up to 85cms
- Size Eight – over 85cms

1. **KOHAKU** – A white Koi with red pattern. This variety is, by far, the most produced and, potentially, the most valuable variety of Koi.

It is also the most difficult variety in which to produce a perfect example hence the reason why the vast majority of Japanese breeders almost always include this variety in their parent stocks.

There is an old saying in Japanese Koi circles that *'We start with Kohaku and finish with Kohaku'*. This generally means that when we come into the hobby there are usually more Kohaku for sale than other varieties and so we buy. Afterwards we become more interested in other – *dare I say?* – 'less boring' varieties.

However, it is only after we have built up experience and then attended serious Koi shows where we can converse with other enthusiasts that the true beauty of Kohaku can really be appreciated.

Below I have included several popular 'pattern styles' of Kohaku as examples only and NOT as requirements.

*Kuchibeni*
*(lipstick pattern)*

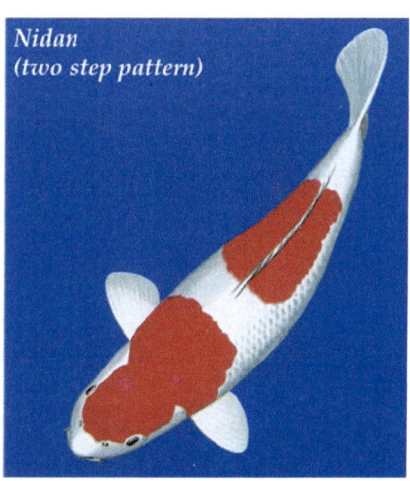
*Nidan*
*(two step pattern)*

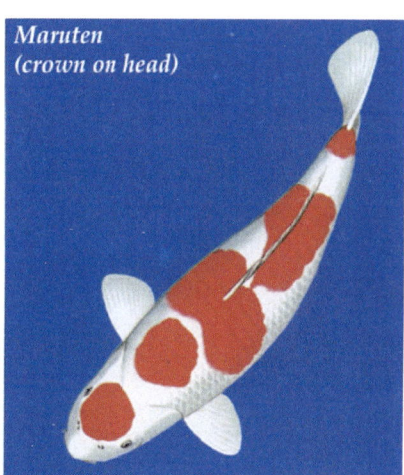
*Maruten*
*(crown on head)*

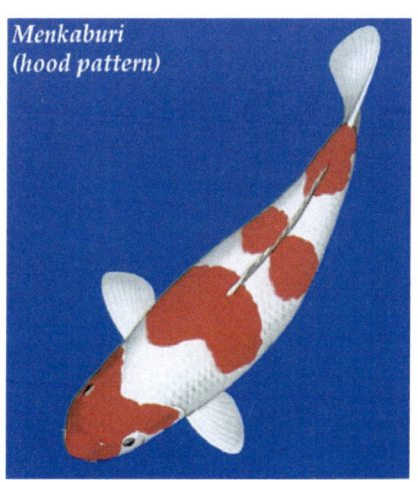
*Menkaburi*
*(hood pattern)*

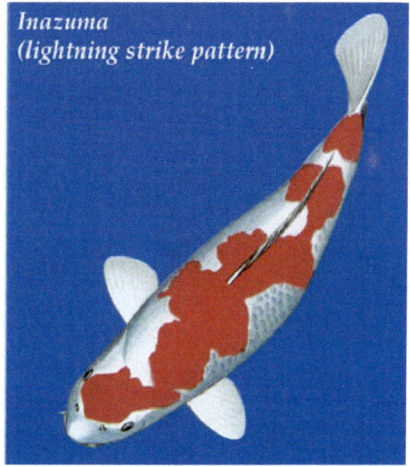
*Inazuma*
*(lightning strike pattern)*

*Yondan*
*(four step pattern)*

2. **SANKE** - A white-based Koi with red and black patterns. This variety is sometimes referred to as 'Taisho Sanke' or 'Taisho Sanshoku'.

It is, probably, the second most desirable variety in Nishikigoi. I have included some popular pattern styles and descriptions below.

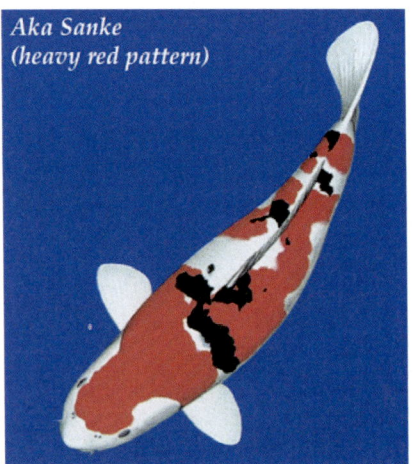

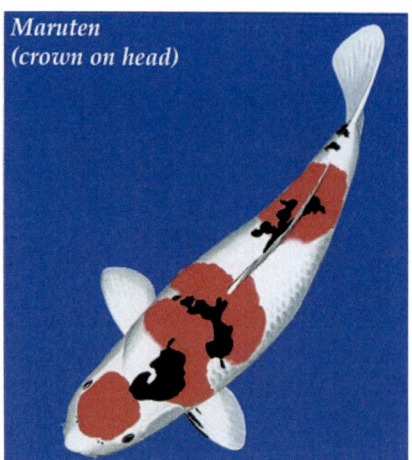

3. **SHOWA** – A black-based Koi with white and red patterns and is also known as 'Showa Sanshoku'. This variety is probably the most popular with both newcomers to the hobby as well as some who have much more experience in Nishikigoi varieties. Again I have included some popular patterns that can be found.

NOTE – Kohaku, Sanke and Showa varieties are collectively known by the term of **'GO-SANKE'** and these are the only varieties that can be considered for 'The Supreme Champion Award' at all major Nishikigoi shows.

4. **TANCHO** – I have included this classification here although it is merely a pattern 'thrown' in the production of the 'Go-Sanke' varieties above. No Japanese breeder actually strives to produce Tancho as such. Again, they are simply random patterns produced and many find them to be very collectable. For entry to Koi shows the 'Tancho Class' is reserved for 'Go-Sanke' varieties only. Other varieties do produce 'Tancho' patterns but these are entered to be judged, in their classifications, alongside the normal patterned entries.

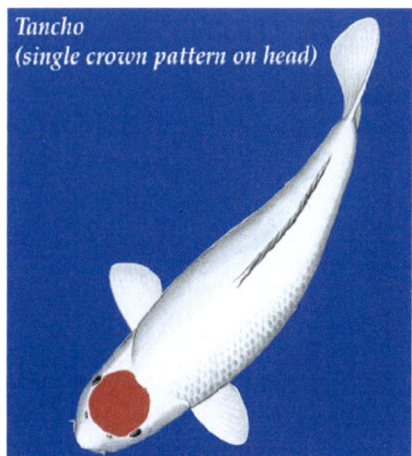
Tancho (single crown pattern on head)

Tancho Showa (single red crown pattern on head)

Tancho (single red crown pattern on head)

5. **BEKKO** – This is also not produced today by any real attempts in Japan. The word Bekko translates as 'tortoise-shell' and I have included here Shiro Bekko – a Sanke without red pattern; Aka-Bekko – a Sanke without white pattern and a Ki-Bekko – a yellow Koi with black pattern - almost impossible to find today.

Shiro Bekko

Aka Bekko

Ki Bekko

6. **'UTSURIMONO'** – These are all derivatives of Showa varieties which have since been produced by intent rather than by accident. Shiro Utsuri is probably the fourth most popular variety for serious enthusiasts after Go-Sanke mentioned before. The word 'Utsuri' in Japan relates to 'change' and these varieties are often subject to pattern changes as they develop. I have included here Shiro Utsuri – a Showa without red pattern; Hi Utsuri – a Showa without white pattern and Ki Utsuri – a black-based Koi with yellow pattern – again, almost impossible to find today.

7. **'KOROMO'** – This is a show classification term given today to Ai-Goromo; Sumi-Goromo; Budo-Goromo; Sumigoromo-Goshiki and Goshiki varieties. I display an example of some of these varieties below.

8. **KIN/GIN RIN'** – *('Gin' is pronounced as in beGIN')* - This is a show classification again reserved only for Go - Sanke varieties of Nishikigoi. All other Kin/Gin Rin Koi are entered to compete with other none Kin/Gin Rin classes in their varieties. 'Kin Rin' refers to Koi adorned with gold reflective scales *(very rare indeed)* and 'Gin Rin refers to the much more common silver reflective scales. These Koi are extremely striking to behold.

9. **ASAGI/SHUSUI** – This classification covers both of these very early varieties.

   Asagi were probably the first true variety of Nishikigoi ever produced whilst Shusui are a 'scale-less' version of Asagi.

   Both of these varieties are still in great demand throughout the world today.

**10. 'HIKARIMUJI'** - Sometimes referred to as 'Hikarimono'. This is a 'classification' for metallic varieties of single colour only *(metallic Matsuba (pinecone) varieties are also included )*. I am including most of the popular varieties below.

**11. 'HIKARIMOYO'** – This is a 'collective term' for metallic varieties of more than one colour *(with the exception of Hikariutsuri which follows)*. Below are some of the more popular varieties that can be found today.

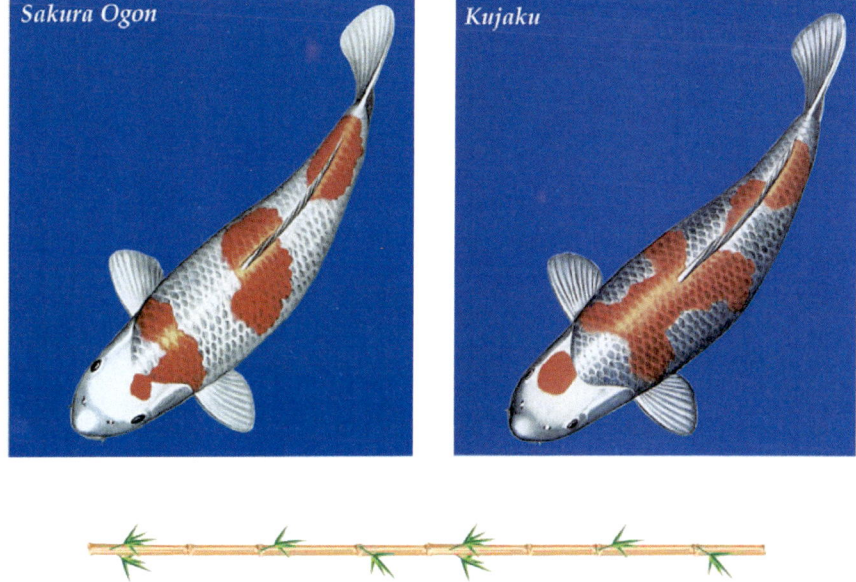

12. **'HIKARIUTSURI'** – These varieties are metallic Koi first developed from Showa varieties, three main examples are displayed below.

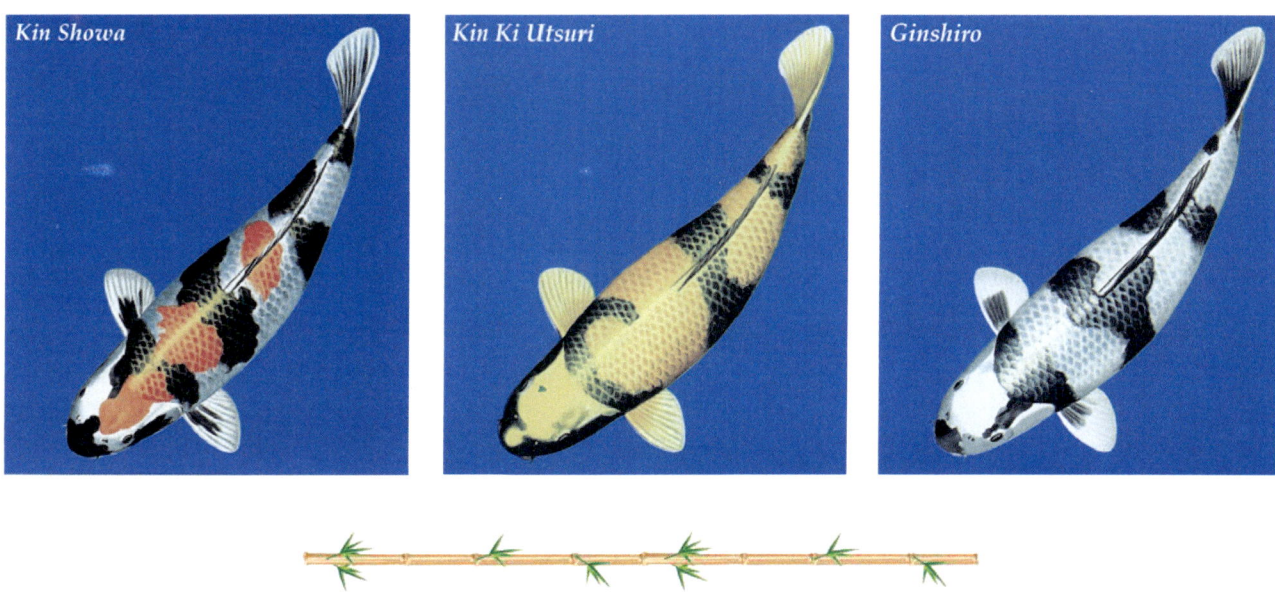

13. **'KAWARIMONO'** – This is an enormous classification for all other non-metallic varieties not covered above. Many of these varieties are extremely popular with enthusiasts around the world. Below are some examples of these varieties.

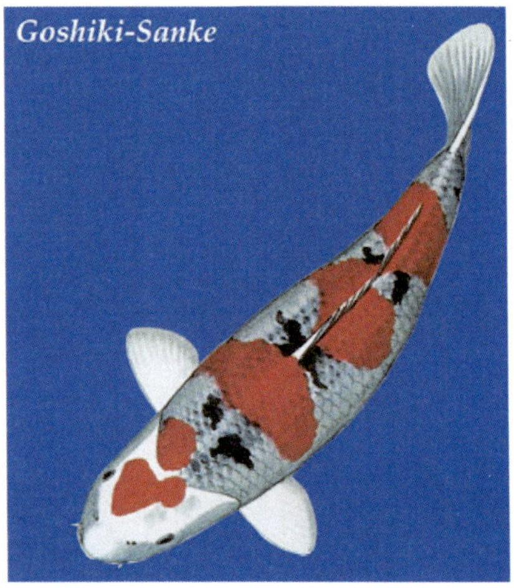

*Goshiki-Sanke*

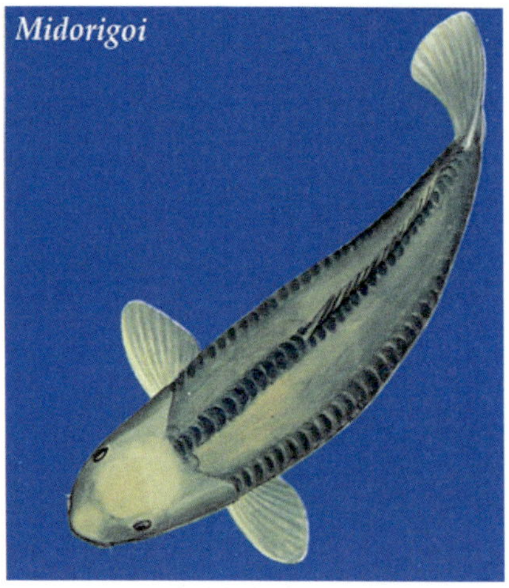

*Midorigoi*

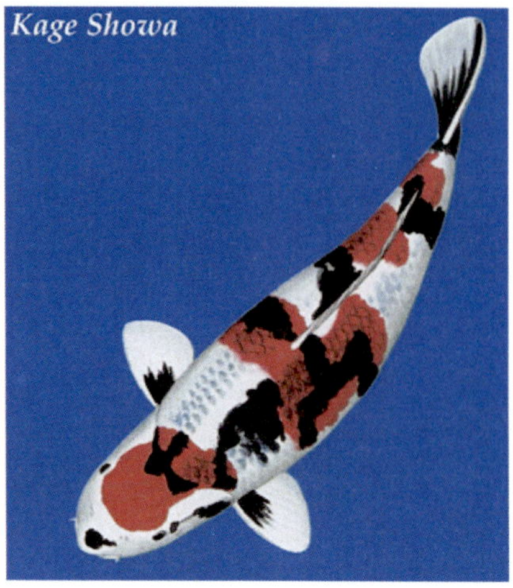

*Kage Showa*

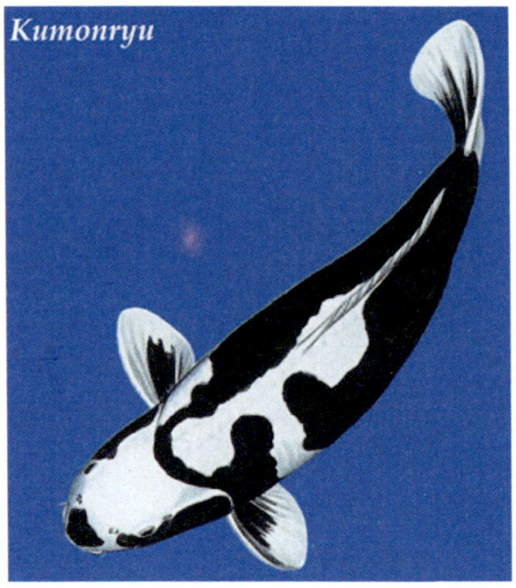

*Kumonryu*

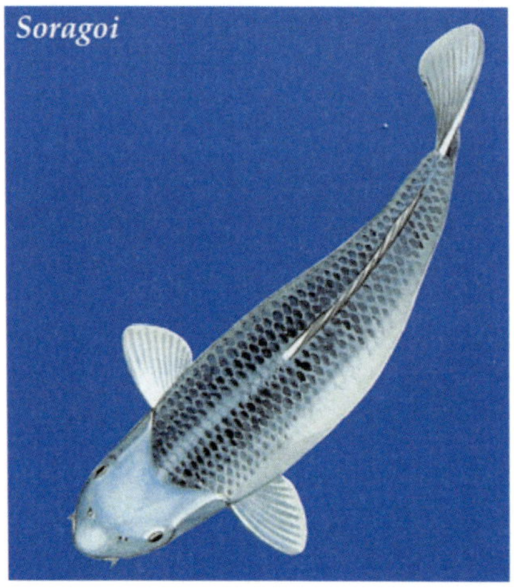

*Soragoi*

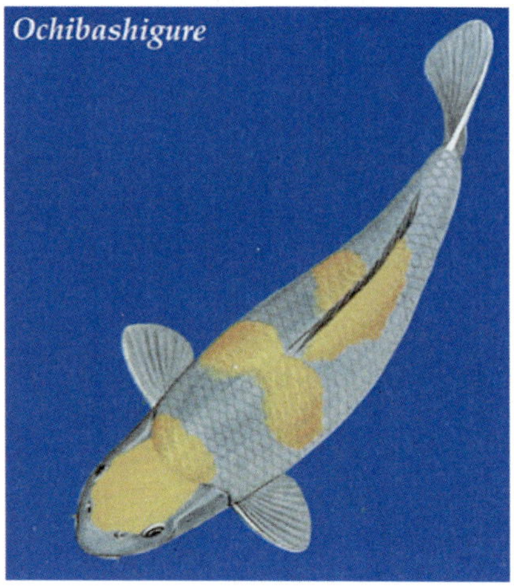

*Ochibashigure*

**14. DOITSU** – Some shows do include Go-Sanke varieties only in this classification whilst non-Go-Sanke varieties must compete in the approprate classes mentioned above. However, there are many shows that do not include this classification which results in all Doitsu varieties having to compete with their fully-scaled *(wagoi)* counterparts. Good examples of these varieties can be extremely beautiful indeed.

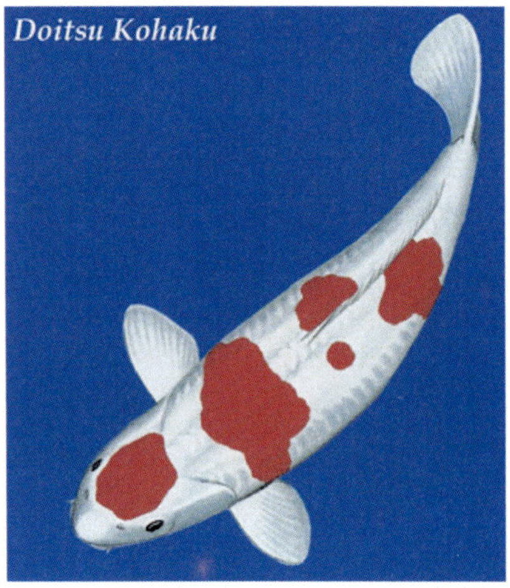

*Doitsu Kohaku*

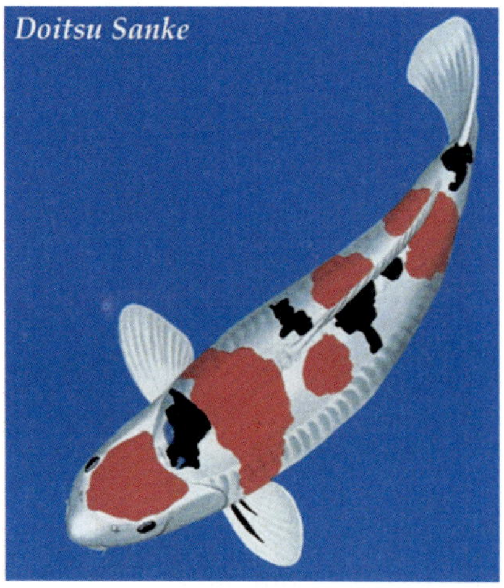

*Doitsu Sanke*

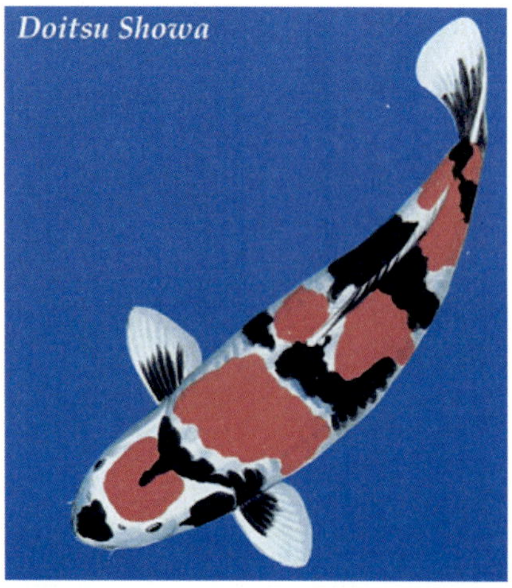

*Doitsu Showa*

- It is almost always that a female Koi takes the major awards at Koi shows as the adult female body shape is much more impressive and desirable than the far slimmer shape of the male.

- Body shape, skin quality, 'frame of the skeleton' and pattern are also very important points to observe in a Koi for show purposes.

- They also can be tamed to feed from the hand thus becoming true family pets. Many collectors also give their Koi pet names!

As to the actual price of Koi, the vast majority of Koi produced are relatively 'cheap and cheerful' as seen in most water garden centres that also stock Koi from other countries as well as Japan.

However some very special Japanese Koi can command very high prices indeed and are usually bought by avid collectors who will enter them into major Koi shows.

During my regular visits to Japan to purchase stocks it is not uncommon to witness a Koi changing hands for 10,000,000yen - £62,000.00 and there are a few other specimens that can command much higher prices.

- All Japanese breeders have limited stocks of their own **'tategoi'** – *(pronounced ta-tay-goy)* which translates as 'Koi which will become better'.

Some of these Koi can command very high prices, even if they are only small in size.

**Japanese breeder lifting a parent Koi from the mud pond to transfer to his indoor heated pond for the winter**

**Tategoi**

The 'quiet and understated' beauty of Kohaku. Nishikigoi such as these specimens are so rare to come across – anywhere in the world and at any time.

The large picture above is a small 45cms, female sansai (three year) Kohaku bred by Masaru Saito in Mushigame village. To produce one single Kohaku with such delicate white ground *(like fragile and priceless porcelain),* then to lay over it the highest quality 'beni' (red pigmentation) possible, and then, to compliment it all with a wonderful and truly unique pattern is the dream of every Nishikigoi breeder in the world today.

# The Koi below are all examples of world-class Nishikigoi as of today, please enjoy!

# 4. THE KOI POND

If possible, your pond should be in view from your house windows in order to maximise the enjoyment from both your pond and your Koi.

**However all garden ponds present a potential danger to both children and pets and this should be taken seriously into account when planning the location and design of your system. Please do bear this in mind.**

As Koi can, and do, grow very large and quite quickly, I suggest the minimum volume for a total Koi system *(pond and filter combined)* should be no less than 2,500 UK gallons or 11.36 tons of water. This equates to *(for example)* a pond of 9 feet by 9 feet by 4.5 feet deep – anything smaller is not really suitable for keeping Koi although many enthusiasts do try and some succeed.

As to the materials to use to build your pond you have a choice here but do bear in mind that Koi thrive best in deep water and one needs a minimum depth of 4 feet (1.23m) but 6 feet (1.84m) is far better.

**This particular system had no direct access for the removal of waste soil so a crane had to be employed to lift the waste skips over the actual house itself!**

The reason for deep water is that Koi are very sensitive to any fluctuations in water temperature. In cold water conditions the Koi will always 'huddle' together at the base of the pond. The water at the base of a deep pond does not fluctuate in temperature nearly as much as the water does in a shallow pond especially when a warm, sunny winter day is followed by a freezing winter night. The water temperature differential here can be quite significant if one bears in mind that a drop of one degree F to humans is equal to a four degrees F drop to a Koi.

There are many different styles of pre-cast plastic or fibreglass ponds available at garden centres which are ideal for keeping goldfish and water plants etc. However, these are not nearly deep enough for keeping Koi properly. They also have no bottom drain facilities built into the pond base for connection to a filter.

### Pre-formed garden ponds

There are also a few deeper, pre-formed plastic ponds available at specialist outlets but very few of these also have the necessary bottom drain facilities which means the system will have to be 'pump-fed'. *(see p28)*

Most of the pre-formed ponds on sale are designed for keeping hardier species of coldwater fish rather than Koi and most reputable retailers will agree.

Another method is by using one of the many waterproof pond liners available and made from various types of plastics through to much stronger butyls. All these have limitations such as:-

- Unsightly creases are present, especially in the corners, when installed - this can harbour a build-up of decaying debris.

- Ground water seepage can 'track' behind the liner which results in significant soil erosion in a deep pond. In severe instances of this, the liner can simply burst. I have witnessed this on several occasions in the past.

- Difficulty in disguising the liner and the final landscaping properly, also some of the cheaper liners are fairly easy to puncture or tear.

### Butyl liner sheet folded

However if you do decide to use a liner for your pond it is worthwhile to note that butyl can be tailored to fit a given pond excavation by having the material 'box-welded' by the manufacturer. This significantly reduces unwanted creases after installation is carried out carefully.

By far the most efficient and strongest method of building a Koi pond is by casting a concrete base and building the 9" thick vertical walls *(no need for shelves to house water plants)* in solid concrete block or solid concrete brick directly onto the base. The blocks are then rendered and sealed with a suitable waterproof membrane such as 'G4' resin or are laminated in GRP (fibreglass). The latter method of final pond waterproofing is favoured by most serious Koi pond enthusiasts for many reasons such as:-

- It is relatively easy to install the bottom drains plus surface skimmer - if required.
- It is relatively easy to install all the return pipe lines correctly.
- It is very easy to landscape.
- Concrete ponds are built to last.

There is no doubt that a concrete construction is by far the best way to build a Koi pond. It may take a little longer to complete and prove a little more expensive to install. However, the results are worth all the extra efforts which outweigh the other available options of pond construction by far.

### Concrete pond ready for render

I'll take a quote of my own from one of my earlier books which is:-

- *'The cheapest possible way to build a Koi pond is to build it once – but build it properly!'*

This maxim still remains accurate today.

There are many shapes of pond to choose from all of which can use different landscaping styles, here are some examples:-

### 'In-ground rock pond'

This 'in-ground rock pond' is my choice of final landscaping on my own pond. These boulders are submerged some 9" below water level and overhang the pond perimeter by some 6" or so in order to create an effect that it is, indeed, 'a natural pond carved out of rock faces'. I built a hidden retaining wall to the rear of the rocks which prevents any water from escaping.

**Left** - The pebble and gravel landscaping completely disguises the retaining wall. *(See p25)*

**Partially above-ground formal pond**

**In-ground formal pond above**

Please try to avoid angular shapes as this produces dead areas that hinder good water circulation which is important in every system. Smooth and curved lines are far more efficient in order to produce good water-return currents which do give valuable exercise to the Koi.

It is also vital in the design stages to roughly estimate the overall volume of the system and to ensure there is available space for the filtration system and other necessary equipment that are covered in detail later.

*(A good method of roughly estimating the final pond volume is to lay a length of string carefully around the outer perimeter of your proposed pond. Next divide the length of the string by four to get a square, multiply the length by the breadth and then multiply by the depth of the pond. If the answer is in cubic feet multiply by 6.23 to get total UK gallons – if the answer is in cubic metres multiply by 1000 to get total litres. This will also give some idea as to the size of the filtration system that will be necessary.)*

## Stages of building a concrete Koi pond.

*(This particular example will be a rectangular pond with finished internal dimensions of 10 feet long by 7 feet wide by 5 feet deep and the final water level will be 2 feet above ground – the filter system will be 'gravity-fed' – important, see below.)*

1. Mark out the area for excavation, in this instance the area will be 11.5 feet long by 8.5 feet wide to allow for the 9" thickness of the pond walls.

2. Note and mark, by string, the final water level which will be 2 feet above ground level.

3. Excavate the entire area to a depth of 4 feet below ground level with vertical walls and a flat base.

4. Cast a 6" deep flat concrete base to the entire area and allow this to cure.

5. Excavate an eight inch wide channel from the pond wall to the filter area to accommodate a 4" bore feed pipe which will link the pond bottom drain to the filter area.

6. Commence to build the pond walls onto the concrete base in either solid concrete blocks (18" x 9" x 4") or concrete common bricks (4.5" x 9" x 4") – the walls are to be 9" thick – leave space for the 4" pipe to exit the pond. Build only three courses of block/brick at this stage.

7. Place the bottom drain on the base of the pond exactly centrally and then solvent-weld the 4" diameter feed pipe into the drain socket. Next connect the 4" diameter pipe along the excavated 8" channel towards the filter area – ensure the pipe and bottom drain are perfectly horizontal to the pond base, you can use stone supports here. Today there are bottom drains available at specialist outlets which also incorporate an air diffuser on the top of the drain itself, this is an ideal way of getting added aeration to the pond without showing unsightly airlines.

8. Cast a second 6" deep, flat concrete base to the pond, this will encase the bottom drain to the level of the top flange and also encase the 4" pipe work. Then allow the base to cure.

9. Continue to build the pond walls to finish 2.5 feet above ground level and 6" above final pond water level. At one corner of the pond wall nearest to the filter build in a 2" bore pipe into the side of the pond wall at around 3 feet above the pond base – later this can be connected to the water return line from the filter and will pump water along one wall of the pond to provide a gentle spin and a vital current to the pond water.

10. Render the entire pond walls with a 0.5" 'scratchcoat' and round off the corners of the pond at the same time. Also form a gentle slope from the pond walls to the perimeter of the bottom drain sump, I suggest a 3" fall from the pond walls to the drain sump in this instance.

11. Next apply a 0.25" smooth, 'trowel finish' render coat to the entire pond.

12. When the pond is totally dry, apply 3 coats of 'G4' resin to seal the entire pond.

A very good alternative here is to have the pond laminated and waterproofed in glass fibre by an experienced contractor.

### GRP laminating

13. Apply 'Paraflex' sealant or similar around the joint between the bottom drain flange and the concrete and also around the 2" return line from the filter. Cut and grind the 2" return line to finish smoothly and flush to the wall of the pond.

14. Once the 4" feed line is connected to the filter and the 2" return line is also connected to the pond. We can now commence to fill the system by using a flow meter on the mains water supply in order to determine the total volume.

15. Clad the concrete blocks/bricks above ground level with stone or a suitable facing brick and finish the pond walls with a suitable coping.

There are two basic methods of supplying pond water to the filtration stages namely:-

   a. **'Pump-Fed'.**

### Basic Pump-fed system
In this method a pump is placed at the deepest part of the pond and water is pumped up into the filter system which is sited higher than the pond water level. Pumped water passes through the filter system and then falls back into the pond by gravity.

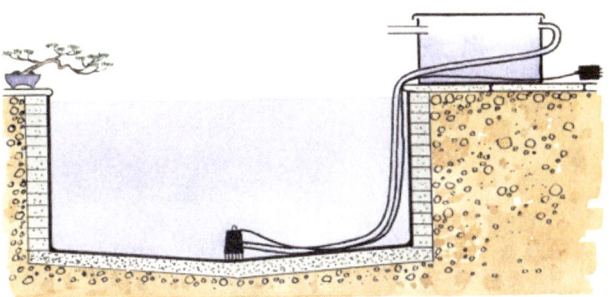

### Improved 'Pump-Fed' system
For those who say a gravity-fed system is not possible in the land available I would seriously consider this option opposite before coming to the final decision. We can successfully incorporate the **vital** bottom drain into the pond base and taking bottom water by gravity to a small concrete

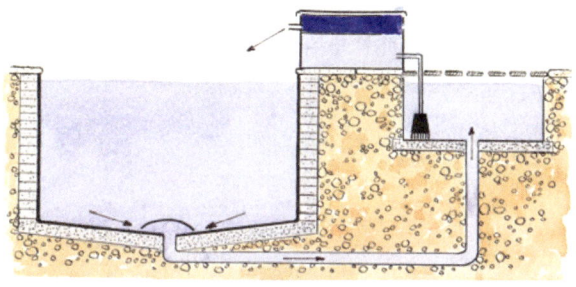

reservoir with water level exactly the same as the pond shown here. In this way there are no unsightly mains cords and flexible tubing in the pond itself. Instead, by placing the submersible water pump into this reservoir as shown, the water can be then supplied to the filter above and exit back to the pond by gravity. The reservoir itself only needs to be large enough to take the submersible pump, mains cord and hose. To improve on this further a drain outlet can be built into the base of the reservoir and capped by standpipe/overflow – this will allow for periodic discharge of the reservoir.

The 'pump-fed' method is now very dated and not recommended at all – *(unsightly pump and pipeline in the pond)* - and not nearly as efficient as the next method because the pump-fed method always requires more maintenance.

However in some rare instances this method has to be employed but regular vacuuming of the pond base will have to be carried out to keep the pond base free from debris and the filter itself will require extra maintenance to prevent excessive blocking.

I would NEVER recommend a 'pump-fed system' to be employed in any Koi pond filter installation.

**Pond Vacuum**

## b. 'Gravity Fed'.

**Gravity-fed system**

This is the method used by most serious enthusiasts today whereby the water level in the pond is exactly equal to the water level in the filters and no unsightly pump or pipe work is visible in the pond. The water exits the pond by gravity and enters

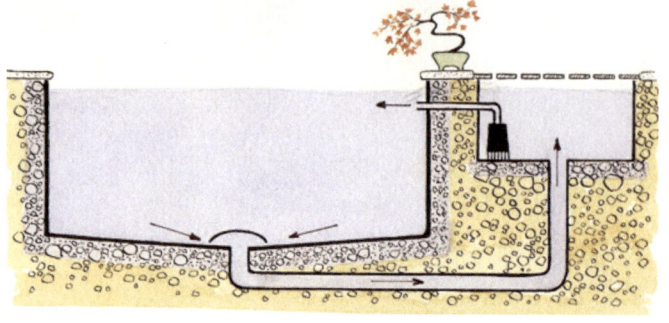

the filter via one or more bottom drains built into the pond base and usually is by way of 4" bore (110mm) pressure tube. The system pump takes water from the last stage of the filter and is then returned to the pond. This causes the level of water in the filter to decrease slightly whilst the water level in the pond accordingly increases slightly. To compensate for these slight variations in levels, water exits the pond via the bottom drain and thus the system operates trouble-free and permanently. There is also no unsightly filter system to be visible above the ground.

**Hand fabricated Bottom Drain**          **Moulded Bottom Drain**

The best bottom drains are hand fabricated in UPVC. There are cheaper injection moulded versions that can be purchased either for concrete ponds or liner ponds.

**'The true Original'**

The units seen on sale today are all derivatives of the original Koi pond bottom drain I first designed and produced for sale back in 1979.

My advice is to always opt for the hand-fabricated UPVC models.

The bottom drain/s take heavy debris – fish waste, mechanical debris and other solids into the first stage of filtration this action also constantly cleans the pond base and thus vacuuming of the base is seldom, if ever, necessary. My own pond has been running constantly for almost ten years and I have never had to vacuum the pond base which always remains totally free from any debris whatsoever.

There are several connections required from both the pond to the filter *(bottom drain feeds)* and from the filter to the pond *(return lines)*. In a liner pond these are made watertight by bottom drain ring flanges and tank connectors. In concrete ponds sealed by 'G4' or laminated by fibreglass the seals are made watertight by using waterproof sealants such as 'Paraflex' or similar silicone products which are non-toxic and are very safe to use in Koi pond applications.

## The real importance of final landscaping.

I have included some styles for final landscaping which may help to to showcase some good designs that are possible to achieve with your own system.

'In-Ground' concrete rock pond

'In and above Ground' unfinished pond

### 'In-Ground' concrete formal pond

Final landscaping is a very personal choice which should hopefully blend in with the area of ground you have available as well as the general style of your home and existing garden. For Koi enthusiasts with a 'flair' for this aspect of Koi keeping, the final results can be really impressive to behold.

Whilst I have mentioned earlier that there is nothing 'natural' as such for our Koi pond system - this does not mean we cannot attempt to make it look as natural as is possible. The hard work put in to create our state-of-the-art system should not be aesthetically compromised with unsightly equipment, wires and pipelines. All of this should be expertly concealed from our eyes instead.

In my own experience, landscaping is a true 'art' form and I have met very few individuals who possess the vital gift of being able to carry it out well.

**The above photograph is from the ability of a landscape professional who has created a true work of art. It gives the impression that these huge boulders have been there, in that very same position, for hundreds of years. In reality, the finished waterfall was less than one year old when this photograph was taken.**

A very acute 'eye' is needed here to be able to visualise, in advance, where every single boulder, each individually trimmed and painstakingly selected, has to be placed in order to produce this final and truly impressive effect.

**Left** - This example demonstrates how a modern and stark concrete bridge design can blend in perfectly with traditional rockwork and gravels.

**Right** - Timber pond edging, large pebbles and huge rocks all contribute to highlight the centrepiece of the ever-popular 'Kaku Yukimi'. *(snow lantern)*

**Left** – An ideal way to landscape the Koi pond into a patio. This shows again how uniform architectural lines can be blended into large rockwork and a waterfall. Water plants are also included in the same water but these cannot be accessed by the Koi.

**Right** – The use of decorative gravels, coloured stones and low conifers can produce a very pleasing and natural effect when landscaped around the rockwork surrounding the pond.

**This is an 'in-ground' formal system I designed for Tom Lansing in Arizona**

# 5. FILTRATION SYSTEMS AND RELATED EQUIPMENT

There are two completely separate types of filtration necessary within a Koi pond system - one is known as '*mechanical filtration*' and the other is known as '*biological filtration*'. In view of this all good Koi pond filters should ideally, for maximum efficiency, have <u>two entirely separate stages</u> incorporated in order to ensure that both types of filtration are adequately catered for. Once this is fully understood it simplifies the basic principles of Koi pond filtration to us all.

**NOTE - Before you hastily put this book back on the shelf I am NOT suggesting you need anything like this one for your Koi pond. But this Koi pond filtration system does exist!**

### a. Mechanical Filtration.

In a Koi pond it is not advisable to include water plants as plants and Koi rarely go together – the Koi forage into the planting baskets and the soil and gravel usually ends up in the pond exactly where we do not want it.

If you really do require water plants I recommend you build an area connected to the pond where your Koi cannot enter.

However it should be pointed out that plants in Koi ponds have no 'natural beneficial properties' in improving water quality at all. They are usually only included for aesthetic purposes and just serve to produce more debris to remove.

There are also many other solid items that are deposited in a plant-free pond such as fish waste – *(Koi produce significant amounts of this)*, leaves, dead algae, dust, un-eaten food etc. etc. These visible items need to be removed from the pond constantly and thence to waste, before they are allowed to build-up and pollute. By taking them into the *mechanical* stage of the filter system and then periodically discharging them to waste we can ensure that all mechanical debris is efficiently removed as is required.

In a 'pump-fed' system - covered earlier, removal of mechanical debris usually means laborious and regular vacuuming of the pond base as the pump only picks up solids from the area around the suction inlet of the pump.

However in a 'gravity-fed' system with correctly sited bottom drain/s, mechanical debris is being removed and taken constantly by gravity into the mechanical stage of the filter and thus, as mentioned earlier, pond vacuuming is generally not necessary at all. Mechanical filtration should always be at the first stage of the filter system and all pond water should pass through this stage before entering the secondary biological stages.

### We do not want any mechanical debris to enter our biological stage/s.

There are several types of mechanical filter available all of which require periodic cleaning by discharging all unwanted solids to waste. As to the actual discharge time periods, these are required more often in warmer water, when feeding is high, than those required in cooler water periods when mechanical debris is not so heavy as a direct result of the lower feeding rates.

Mechanical filter stages can be by way of settling chambers; brush chambers; vortex units and static media methods.

1. **Settling chambers** – these are merely water containers without any filter media which receive the water directly from the pond at a gentle flow rate and coaxes heavier solids to settle out on the base before passing through to the biological stages.

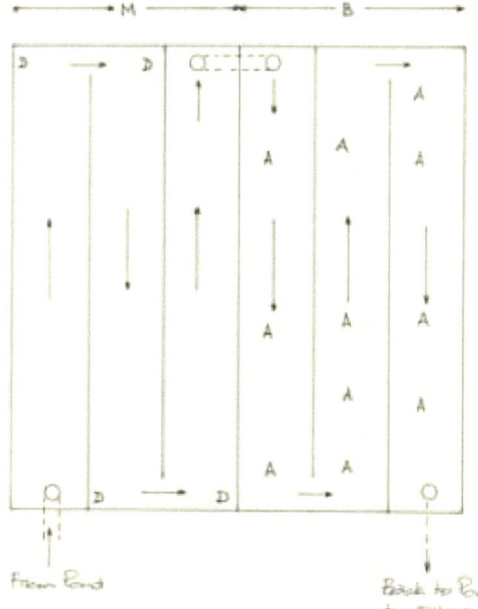

Please excuse my very rough sketch here but I think this design is important especially to those where available space is no problem.

It is, in fact, a superb and very simple **'settling filter'** where no actual media is involved as such. I have not given any dimensions as this will vary depending on the volume of water to be filtered but instead I have just outlined the principle of the idea.

The container is relatively shallow and is fed by gravity from the pond drain and returned to the pond as shown. The filter itself is just a series of narrow and long 'canals' where water flow passes through freely and horizontally. The three canals marked 'M' are the mechanical stages where the walls and base are finished in smooth render. The three canals marked 'B' are the biological stages where the walls and base are finished in rough 'Canterbury Spar' pebble dash and this is where excellent biological filtration will take place. Water is transferred from mechanical stage to biological stage via the two sockets connected underground as shown. 'D' denotes where the direction change of water flow provides the most settling out of heavy solids. 'A' denotes areas of very heavy aeration throughout the biological canals. Drains for discharge can be added to both mechanical and biological stages for disposal of waste water to the sewer.

**2. Brush chambers** – the simple settling chamber described above can be made to work far more efficiently by adding vertical rows of crimped polypropylene filter brushes as a 'barrier' for water flow entering into the chamber.

This, in turn, stops much more debris from entering the biological stages. Periodically, as required, the brushes are quickly cleaned by garden hose and all mechanical debris can easily be flushed to waste.

**3. Vortex units** – these units are available in many sizes which depend on the volume of water to filter and the required flow rates. They are usually made from GRP (glass fibre) and are tall, circular chambers which narrow to a coned base. These can be very efficient, if fed correctly, in taking, by 'centripetal action', mechanical debris to the bottom of the cone for easy and periodic discharge to waste by a valve installed at the base of the cone.

Sadly, all too often we find vortex units which are far too small for the flow rate necessary

which results in a 'spin' that is far too fast and debris has no time to settle out. An ideal vortex set-up is one which is large enough to produce a very gentle spin *(dictated by the flow-rate)* which will induce the solids to settle within the cone of the chamber for periodic discharge to waste via a suitable ball valve.

**These are four 'banks' of vortex units in my own filter house showing drains from each one taken into the main discharge box built into the floor.**

**4. Static media containers** – in these systems all pond water entering into the mechanical stage has to pass through a deep bed of static media before it is allowed to exit into the biological stage of the filter.

Debris is simply trapped within the static media *(usually plastic)* and periodically the media can be back-washed by heavy aeration which is built into the base of the chamber or by water pressure *(heavy rinsing)* alone. Fouled water and mechanical debris is then discharged to waste quickly and efficiently. I am not completely convinced by this form of 'strainer' and prefer to adopt the simpler methods covered earlier.

5. Recently several manufacturers have produced '**sieves**' as a prime mechanical filter – see opposite. These generally work quite well in separating solids from the entry water, especially fine strands of algae. They are available in both plastic and metal containers and generally require installation by a professional as levels must be exact.

As with all forms of mechanical filtration they do require periodic cleaning but, on the whole, they work very well.

6. There are other mechanical filters on the market such as bead filters and sand filters as used on swimming pools and these do 'trap' mechanical debris. All these systems require regular discharge by way of tiresome back-washing coupled with severe wastage of good water. I also often wonder just how much of the debris is actually disposed of by this method.

## b. Biological filtration.

Koi, by way of gill action and urine, produce toxic ammonias which are dissolved into the pond water. If these are allowed to build up within the system they can prove to be fatal to Koi stocks. As these toxins are completely dissolved within the water, no mechanical filtration stages can remove them. Instead we must pass them through the biological stages across and through 'surfaces' of media which, when mature, are home to a biomass formed by healthy aerobic bacteria that rely on the ammonias in the water as their sustenance.

Once a biological stage is fully mature, this results in the bacteria taking in the dissolved toxin as their food source. This then results in the Koi depending on the bacteria in the filter to provide them with 'good toxin-free water' and also the bacteria within the filter relying on the toxins produced by the Koi for their 'food' – and so the cycle continues, just as long as the water circulation remains constant.

**To summarize – in a mature re-circulating system the bacteria in the filter rely on the Koi for their food and the Koi rely on the bacteria for good, purified water.**

**This is more commonly referred to as 'The Nitrification Process'.**

The ammonia is then converted by the bacteria, firstly into toxic nitrites and thence into non-toxic nitrates before being returned to the pond. This takes place in all biological stages and varies from being mildly efficient to being very efficient depending on flow patterns, retention time and the actual choice of biological media within the filter.

### 'New pond syndrome'

*Here is a good place to describe this phenomenon which affects ALL new ponds. After a system has been completed and some Koi are added, things seem to be perfectly normal for the first few days when the Koi can be seen feeding and behaving normally.*

*However the media surfaces in the biological stages are not as yet mature enough to support the bacteria which need time to form with the introduction of the ammonia from the Koi. As a result the ammonia content is returned to the pond water and the next stage produces a nitrite build-up in the pond water also.*

*The ammonia and nitrite contents need to be 'dissolved' by the addition of fresh water by carrying out ample water changes. Also reductions in feeding should be made in order to allow the bacteria to begin to process their source of 'food'.*

**This is an important reason as to why all Koi ponds should incorporate a system overflow to waste as this allows new water to be added and unwanted pond water and rainwater to be removed without flooding the garden.**

*Maturing of a system which is suffering from 'new pond syndrome' usually takes around six to seven weeks – this can be accelerated by adding mature media from another system.*

*Obviously, a system cannot begin to mature without fish stocks added to 'kick-start' the nitrification process.*

There is a wide choice of media available to provide a healthy biomass of bacteria to the surfaces within the biological stages of Koi pond filtration. In fact, any inert and non-toxic surface will support a biomass.

- The efficiency of filtration can be greatly assisted by the very important addition of heavy aeration by air stones to the biological stages of the filter in order to give more dissolved oxygen content which is eagerly consumed by the biomass.

As already mentioned, just about any non-toxic submerged media can support bacteria after the maturing process has been completed and all vary in degrees of efficiency but here are some favoured by many experienced Koi keepers:-

**1. Filter mat cartridges** – these are supplied and fabricated from 2m x 1m X 3cms porous flat sheets of polyester material imported from Japan and can be tailored to fit any given chamber exactly. These can be used in either 'upward-flow' or 'horizontal-flow' applications and the cartridges are formed into a series of 3cm 'square channels' which allows the heavily aerated water to pass through them with no restriction whatsoever. The biomass is then allowed to develop and then reproduce on the vast surface area provided by all the surfaces of the cartridges. After a cartridge has been formed, it is fastened securely together on the outside by plastic banding tape *(no glue required)*. Should the need ever arise, the cartridge can simply be lifted out and briefly hosed down before replacement.

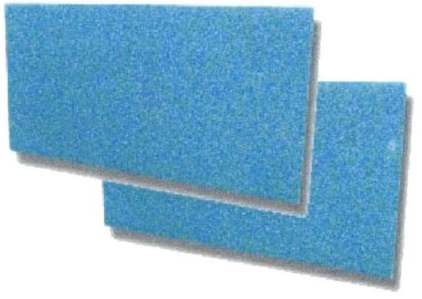

**Japanese filter matting sheets**

This material is the prime biological media choice of many enthusiasts in the UK and most Nishikigoi breeders in Japan. I introduced this material into the UK in 1985 after being shown working examples in use at many breeder's facilities in Japan. I have used this exclusively, together with heavy aeration, on my own systems ever since – with perfect results. This has, long since, been the media of my choice.

**Cutting filter mat cartridges with a knife blade**

**NOTE:- Please do ensure you purchase the genuine material which is imported from Japan and lasts indefinitely. There are several cheaper European versions of this which do not last for long when submerged.**

2. **'Moving Bed' media** – this is a plastic, semi-floating type of media which is buoyant in the water. The media has been adopted by many enthusiasts in recent years. When heavy aeration is added underneath the media, the entire bed 'boils' with activity. The bacteria form on the inside and outside of all its surfaces, and,

in a mature system, dead bacteria are constantly falling off to make way for more new biomass to form.

This media, however, poses a minor problem in that it has to be contained and then prevented from escaping into any further biological stages by the use of old-style perforated UPVC sheet. It is, in fact, an 'aerated modernisation' of the use of hair curlers and chopped plastic corrugated pipe commonly seen and used in Koi pond filters during the mid 1980's.

3. **Gravels and other 'solid bed' media** – these can be used in an 'upward-flow' situation but are seldom used nowadays as blockages usually occur at some point which necessitates laborious periodic cleaning and significant loss of biomass which only forms on the top $3/8^{th}$ of an inch of the surface.

*NB - It should be obvious to see here that the Koi are producing ammonia through urine and gill action all year round and the bacteria within the filter are also reproducing all year round. In view of this one should **never** completely turn off the filter system in winter as many do still advocate. In recent times, there are some enthusiasts who have mature filter systems and they experiment with both reduced flow rates and automatic on/off timers during cold water periods. Either or both of these methods can reduce electricity costs significantly.*

Finally, on the subject of biological filtration, once again, we are not attempting to 'strain out' any mechanical debris in these stages. Instead we are simply passing water through and across the biological surfaces to feed the biomass with dissolved, toxic ammonias.

## Choice of filter system

This has to be made when the volume of the pond itself has been decided upon. A small volume system can run on a much smaller sized filter than the filter required on a larger volume system. Also do remember that there will be other items to plan for when estimating filter size such as places to house the items of equipment *(covered below)* - ultra-violet clarifier; water pump; air pump; heater etc. All these need to be taken into acount to be easily accessible for periodic cleaning and/or servicing.

There are many 'off-the-shelf filter systems' available, all professing to filter a given volume of water. These range from simple domestic cold water header tanks *(which I suggest you avoid if you wish to keep Koi)* through to large fibreglass or plastic units in dozens of different makes, shapes and sizes.

**Ready-made filter systems**
Here the newcomer is in a minefield as to making the correct choice. In my experience it is always best to err on the side of safety here and buy a filter that will filter your water volume 'twice over'.

*(For example, if your pond is 3,000 gallons, buy a filter that claims to be able to filter 6,000 gallons just to be on the safe side!)*

I have come across many such claims in the past. <u>Please remember, it is not possible to 'over-filter' your pond but it is very easy to 'under-filter' your pond!</u>

Also do make sure that these units incorporate both good mechanical and biological stages of filtration – if not, then find one that does!

- *However, it should be firmly pointed out here that garden centres and water garden centres do also cater for many different kinds of pond fish keeping. Pre-formed ponds, liners and 'black box' filters all have a real place here to keep varieties which are far more hardy than are Koi. If you explain that it is Koi you wish to keep then I am sure they will steer you to more suitable items of equipment.*

**Old-style gravel filter system on the roadside in Koguriyama village, still in use today!**

### Alternatively, one can build one's own filter system.

The following filter systems have been tried and tested over many years. They perform superbly and can be easily and cheaply constructed, save the last one where a vortex unit has to be purchased. The biological stages of these three systems operate on a 'horizontal-water flow' principle and, although very simple in operation, produce truly excellent biomass. They can be built easily from solid concrete blocks and finished, after rendering, with a suitable waterproof coating such as 'G4' resin. The principles of these systems will be detailed later.

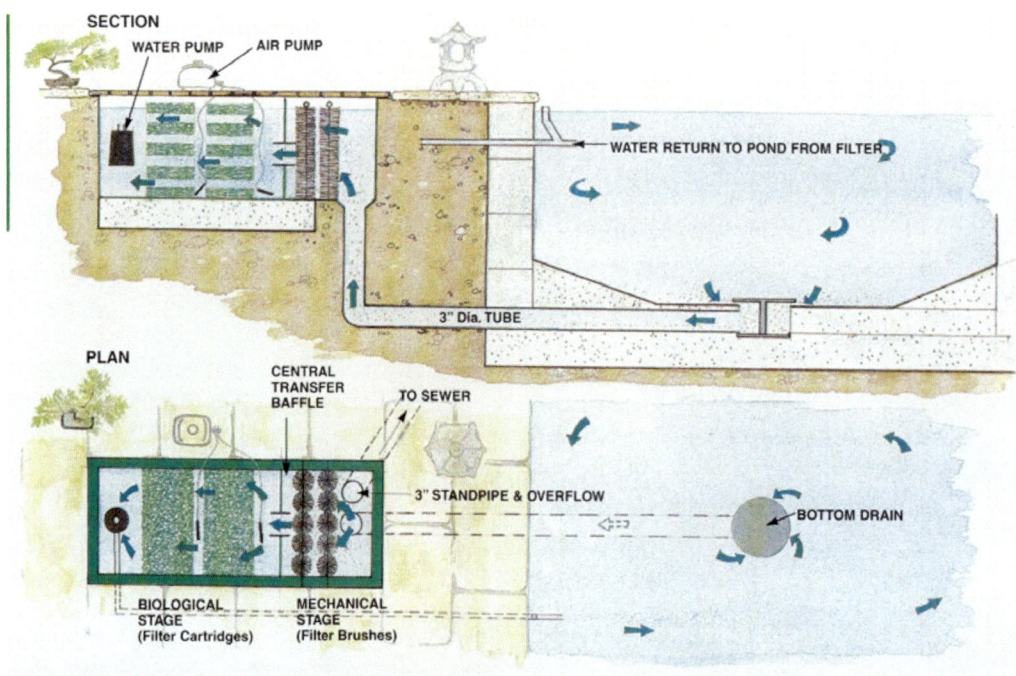

**1. This filter is perfect for a small system of up to 1,250 UK gallons (5.68 tons)**

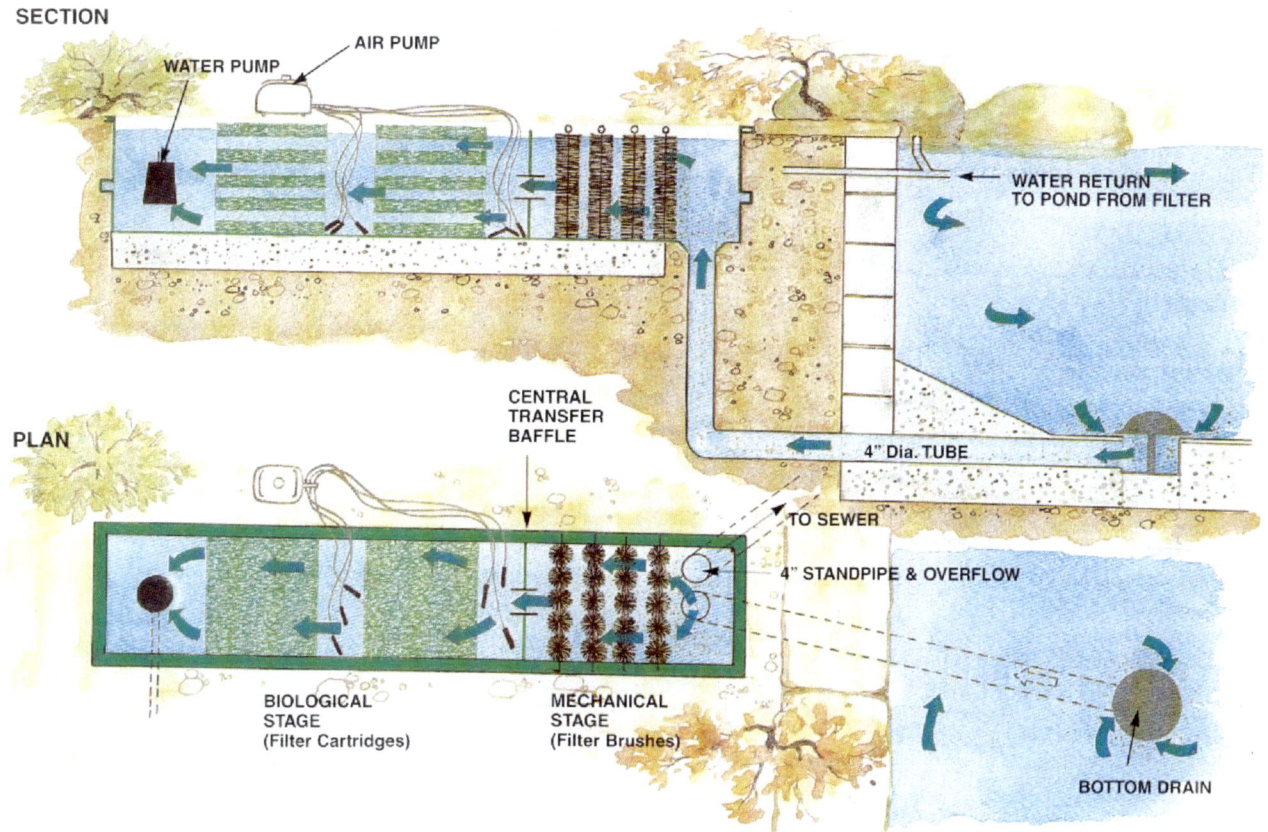

**2. This design is for a system of 2,500 UK gallons (11.36 tons!**

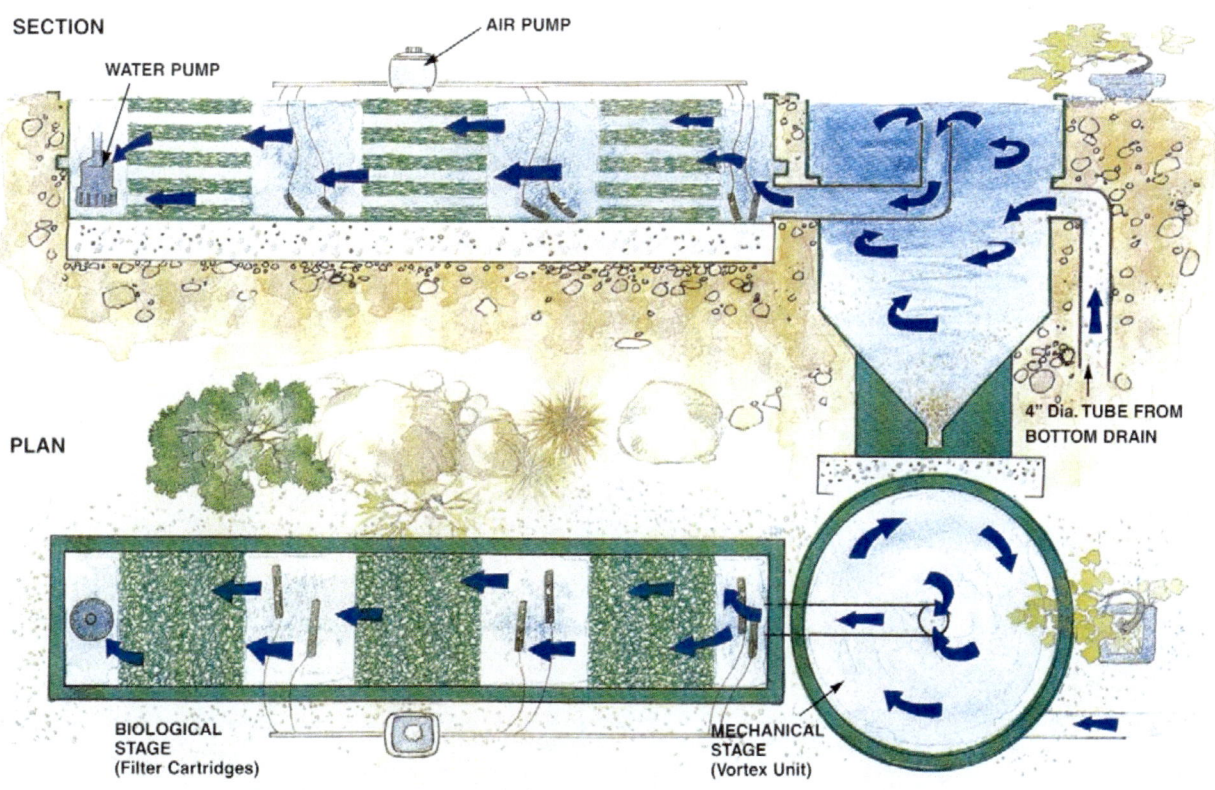

**3. This system is designed to handle 3,750 UK gallons (17.05 tons)**

I have detailed and illustrated in the 'Pond' section above, the differences between 'Pump-Fed' and 'Gravity-Fed' systems. I have also detailed and illustrated in this section the principles and requirements of both 'Mechanical' and 'Biological' aspects of a Koi pond filtration system.

I will now attempt to simplify and clarify all the previous information I have given.

The modern-day Koi pond incorporates the following seven items:-

1. **The Pond.** This is simply a water-retaining structure designed to house our Koi and allow a good water-flow or recirculation pattern by proper design.

2. **The Bottom Drain/s.** This is/these are - simply the link from the pond to a filter. A bottom drain is installed at the deepest part of the pond with the pond base gently sloped towards the sump of the drain. A bottom drain operates permanently to ensure that all mechanical debris and 'heavier-than-water-ammonias' are taken out of the pond constantly and into the filter system.

3. **The Filter System.** This also is simply a water-retaining structure – nothing more and nothing less. In short it is merely a 'container' which should firstly provide excellent 'mechanical filtration' by the efficient removal of all debris coming into the filter from the bottom drain/s and should not allow any of this debris to pass into the next stage. Secondly the media inside the filter should provide excellent and efficient 'biological filtration' which will remove the dissolved toxins covered earlier and prevent them from being returned to the pond. If there is any 'magic' at all – which there isn't, it is purely in the efficiency of the mechanical 'barriers' and the efficiency of the biological media in question. Once again, the 'box' itself *(no matter what shape or what colour or what it is made of)* is merely a 'box' and this is very important to bear in mind. I will elaborate on this later in much greater detail.

4. **The Pump** *(below).* This item brings 'the heartbeat of the entire system' into life and obviously, without this, there will be no system circulation at all.

5. **The Ultra-Violet System** *(below).* This is employed only to remove 'green water' or to prevent this from taking place in the first instance. It has nothing at all to do with filtration. It does not destroy blanket weed or floating algae nor does it eradicate any parasites or bacteria. *(As an aside here, Koi keepers generally wish to remove green water in order to see their Koi clearly, however 'good green water' conditions are absolutely superb in improving lustre, pigmentation and overall health of our Koi. Alas, it is very difficult to provide and control good green water permanently although many of us have tried.)*

6. **The Heating System** *(below).* Some form of heating should be incorporated into every system even if this is almost never to be used. Our Koi are valuable both as pets as well as in monetary terms. If the keeper is faced with a sudden and severe drop in water temperature which could be harmful to the Koi then built-in heating will be available to be quickly employed to resolve the matter and keep the Koi safe.

7. **Aeration** *(below).* This is absolutely vital for both pond dissolved oxygen content and in the biological stage of the filter in order to give this vital element to the biomass by way of the heavily aerated water passing through.

**These seven items should be linked together as follows:-**

    A. <u>**In a standard 'pump-fed' system**</u> as described above, this is –

POND ➡ PUMP IN POND ➡ U/V CLARIFIER ➡ HEATER ➡ FILTER and then back to the pond by gravity.

    B. <u>**In a 'pump-fed with bottom drain' system**</u> described above, this is -

POND ➡ BOTTOM DRAIN ➡ EXTERNAL PUMP CHAMBER ➡ PUMP ➡ U/V CLARIFIER ➡ HEATER ➡ FILTER and back to the pond by gravity.

    C. <u>**In a 'gravity-fed' system**</u> as described above, this is –

POND ➡ BOTTOM DRAIN ➡ FILTER ➡ PUMP ➡ U/V ➡ HEATER ➡ and then back to the pond.

I have seen and often used, over many years, just about every form of Koi pond filtration principles and designs - that have been available, and some that still are today.

<u>However, I must admit that I still fail to be even slightly impressed by what is currently on offer - anywhere.</u>

**My main reason is simply because I need a filtration system that doesn't conceal anything I cannot readily and constantly see with my own two eyes – is that really too much to ask for in this day and age?**

In view of this I must immediately discount any form of 'sealed and enclosed systems' at all. This includes sand filters and 'bubble-bead' filters and all their many derivatives. *(Over the years I have broken some of these systems apart to find a putrifying mess of constantly decaying and very 'smelly' sludge – totally alien to the claims made by the manufacturer who has long-since stopped caring or has even ceased to trade.)*

My own choice of filter system needs **'to be'** and **'to be seen'** as 'squeaky-clean' as is my pond – and that means always!

Do I need a depth of plastic mechanical static media bed crammed on top of each other that I am told will be <u>totally cleaned</u> by simply employing heavy aeration below it? Sorry, unless I can see this, with my own two eyes, that this is so, I will choose simply not to believe it. This then requires that the entire static bed is laboriously removed by bucket and a scoop, to actually witness 'if' or 'if not' the claims made are accurate. The 'static-bed principle' is seriously flawed as it is no different to any other mechanical stage at all - ie. It has to be cleaned thoroughly – and by hand – if it is to be cleaned <u>properly</u>.

As to the biological stages readily available for purchase, I am not the slightest bit impressed in seeing 'lumps of plastic dancing around in front of my eyes'. Instead I wish to see just what is happening **below** all of this. Again, I cannot see this and thus will continue **not** to believe it.

Bearing in mind the above, what are my own recommendations in order to supply the very best forms of mechanical and biological filtration to a Koi pond in 2009? One thing is certainly true and that is - there is nothing new to call upon in this subject and there has not been for many years. <u>If there was, please have no doubts at all, the Japanese Koi breeders would be the very first to adopt it.</u>

In view of all this, I must return, yet again, to the use of a filter container *(of specified and exact size)* which will hold - Mechanical Media of Filter brushes and Biological Media of heavily-aerated tailored Japanese Filter mat cartridges incorporated within a Horizontal-Flow pattern. This is exactly the same type of filtration I first published in 1995 in my book 'Koi Kichi' together with the odd improvement made since then.

**'Old Hat'!** – some may say, but I don't think so, not even in the slightest.

Please allow me to explain why this method of Koi pond filtration is as 'up-to-the-minute' as is possible in 2009.

As an example I will use system 2 above which is for 2,500 UK gallons – but I know from experience that this can easily cope with 3,200 UK gallons. As the drawing shows, this is an in-ground, gravity-fed system which will be a home-made filter container built from solid concrete blocks onto a concrete base.

**Excavation required** – In this example I will assume that the final water level will be 6" (15cms) below the existing flat ground and the filter walls will continue a further 6" (15cms) to finish at ground level. The outside wall thickness will be 6" (15 cms) and the concrete base will be 4" (110ml) thick. The filter itself will have internal dimensions of 9 feet long (2.7 metres) – 20" wide (51 cms) and 20" (51 cms) deep to the final water level. We must add to this depth a further 4" (10 cms) for the concrete base and a further 6" (15 cms) to bring the filter wall up to ground level. The total excavation therefore required for all this will be 10 feet long (3.08 metres) – 32" wide (81 cms) and 30" (75 cms) deep. The total ground excavation in this example will be a mere 66.5 cubic feet or 1.82 cubic metres of soil – please bear this in mind.

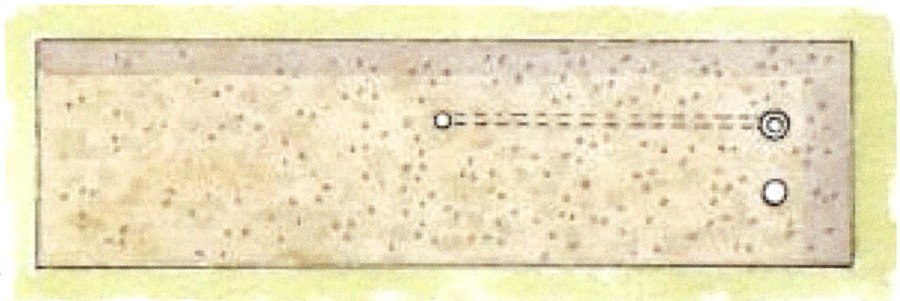

**Plan of excavation – see above text for dimensions**

**Concrete base details** – before the base is cast, there are three fittings to incorporate in the soil and these are shown in the plan below which are as follows:-

a. One 4" (110ml) socket to finish 4" (110ml) above the base of the excavation. This will be connected to the 4" (110ml) pipe line from the bottom drain and serves as the water supply to the filter.

b. One 4" (110ml) socket to finish 4" (110ml) above the base of the excavation. The underside of this socket will be reduced to 2" (50ml) for connection to the mains sewer for discharge/overflow water.

c. One 2" (50ml) socket and tube to finish 4" (110ml) above the base of the excavation. This will be connected underground to the 2" (50ml) pipe line mentioned in 'b' above and this will also be used to discharge water to waste.

Before the 4" (110ml) concrete base is finally cast, do protect the tops of all three sockets with short lengths of tube to prevent concrete from entering these sockets. Once the base has been cast the top of the base and the tops of the three sockets will be completely flush.

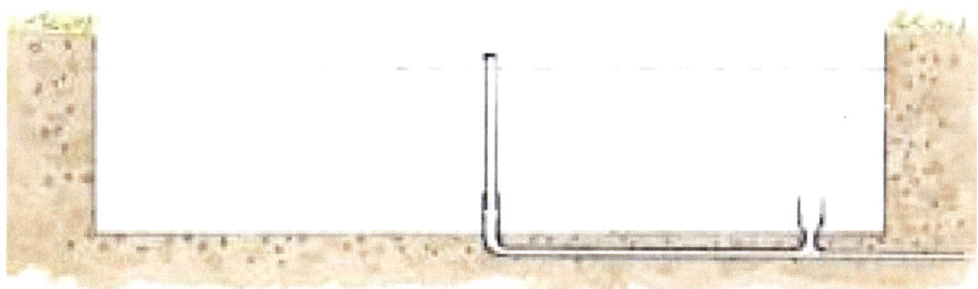

**Section of excavation showing pipe installations described above**

**Construction details** - once the base has cured, the four outer walls can be built in 6" (15cms) blockwork right up to ground level.

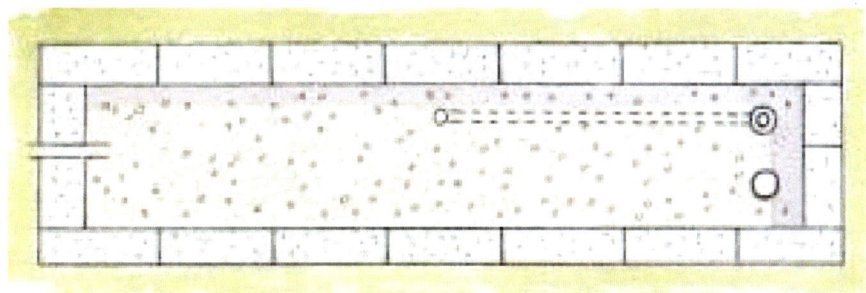

**Plan showing base cast and walls built, the tops of the three sockets are now level with the top of the concrete base.**

We now build a 4" (110ml) thick brick wall inside the filter and this will separate the prime mechanical section from the biological section. This will be built as per the drawing below and will be exactly 24" (60cms) from the start of the filter. During the building of this wall a 4" (110ml) short length of pressure tube should be built into it at dead centre of the wall and this can be trimmed later. This pipe will transfer water flow centrally from the mechanical stage into the biological stage.

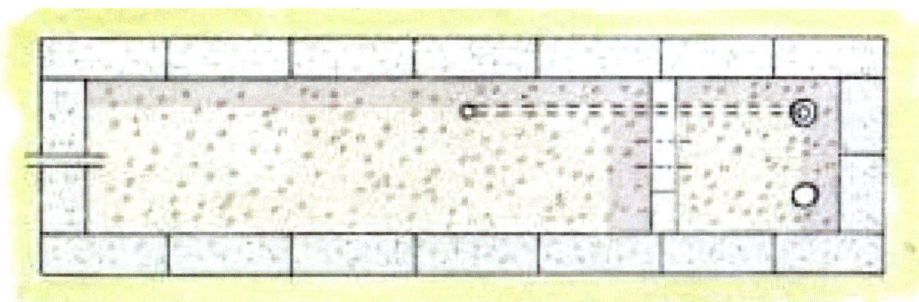

**Dividing wall built showing transfer tube linking the mechanical stage to the biological stage.**

Once this has all been completed, the entire internal walls of the filter, including the divider wall can be rendered with a 0.5" trowel finish. After this has cured, the entire walls of the filter can be given three coats of 'G4' resin (or a GRP lamination) in order to ensure the chamber is fully watertight. Once sealed it is important to use a non-toxic silicone sealant around each of the tops of the three sockets and to both sides of the transfer tube in the divider wall to ensure no seepage will take place between the plastic and the waterproofing. After this, the transfer tube can be carefully trimmed to be flush with the divider wall on both sides. The container is now complete and should be filled with water to ensure it is totally watertight but this can only be done after the three sockets have been stopped temporarily with adjustable rubber pipe stops available from plumber's supply outlets and we will need these later on.

**Installing the filter media** – the width of the mechanical stage is 20" (51cms) and we require four rows of five crimped filter brushes (20 in total) to be suspended as close to the transfer tube as is possible. These brushes should be 4" (110ml) diameter and 20" (51ml) long. They should form a barrier right across the width of the filter. We now need three tailored, horizontal-flow Japanese filter mat cartridges cut for the biological stage. These will each be 20" (51cms) deep, 20" (51cms) wide and 18" (45cms) long. After these have been completed they are firmly banded in two places with plastic banding strips for easy placement and removal.

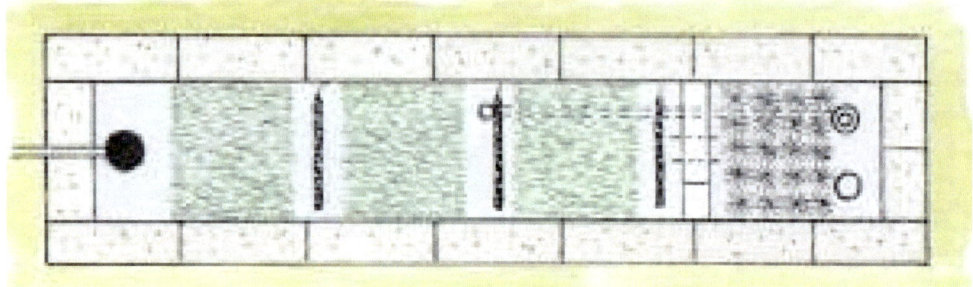

**Plan view of the finished filter showing media and points of aeration**

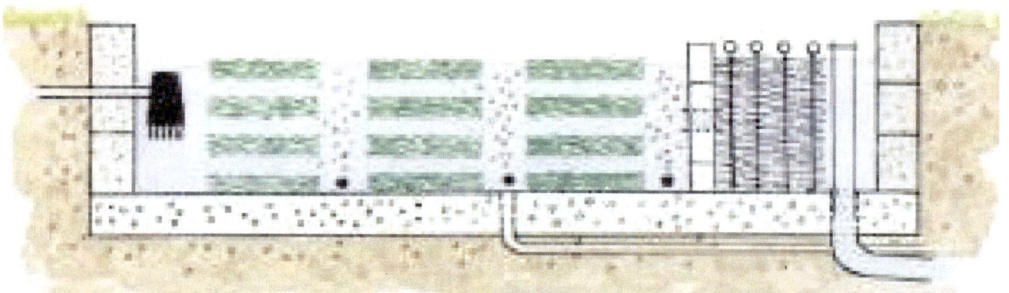

**Section view of finished filter showing pipelines**

**Standpipes required** – these can be fabricated by UPVC specialist companies and should not be expensive to purchase. I would suggest you purchase two of each and keep one of each as a spare. They are made by welding a normal length of standard tube to a small section of 'thick-wall' tube. The 4" (110ml) standpipe we need for this system would be a 4" (110ml) length of thick-wall tube welded to a 22" (56cms) length of standard 4" (110ml) tube. The 2" (50ml) standpipe we need will be a 3" (90mm) length of thick-wall tube welded to a 22" (56cms) length of standard 2" (50mm) tube. Once these have been completed, the fabricator can insert a pull handle in solid UPVC rod to the tops of the standpipes and then turn a groove in the thick wall parts of the tube which will accommodate the 1/4" rubber 'O' ring. This 'O' ring rubber can easily be obtained from DIY suppliers, cut to size and held firmly together with 'super glue'. On using the standpipes for the first time it is well to give the rubber seals a thin coat of 'Vaseline' or similar, after this they will insert and remove perfectly. Once the 4" (110ml) standpipe is in position and the system is running at normal level, mark the water level on the side of the standpipe. After this, drill a series of ¼" holes just above this mark, this serves as an ideal overflow for the total system.

**Running and discharge operation** – in normal running position, the 4" standpipe is placed in the socket which connects the filter to the sewer and the socket coming from the drain is left open. The 2" standpipe is placed firmly into its socket and the central tube in the divider wall is open. Very heavy aeration is supplied to the biological stage where indicated. This not only provides vital aeration to the surfaces on the filter cartridges – it also 'disturbs' the flow pattern of the water to ensure all surfaces obtain a constant supply of layered horizontal water flow. We now have before us a filter system whereby every single part can be clearly seen before us, there are no 'hidden' secrets whatsoever. <u>In short, EXACTLY as I want it to be!</u>

The discharge of the mechanical stage, as and when required, is as follows:- Stop the main water pump ➡ place a 4" pipe stop into the transfer tube in the division wall *(this isolates the mechanical stage from the biological stage)* ➡ take the 4" standpipe from its socket and immediately place it into the socket which enters the mechanical stage from the bottom drain *(this isolates the pond from the filter and also empties all the water in the mechanical stage to waste)* ➡ hose down all the brushes with a strong water jet from a garden hose and then replace them *(all the debris and waste water will be taken to the sewer)* ➡ take the standpipe from the bottom drain feed and replace it in the socket to the sewer *(the mechanical stage will now fill completely)* ➡ remove the pipe stop from the dividing wall ➡ switch on the main pump and the system is running again as normal. The entire procedure takes less than five minutes.

As to periodic cleaning of the biological stage, this is rarely necessary and only is required if one can see any visible debris in this section of the filter. If this is required from time to time the procedure is as follows:- Stop the main water pump ➡ place a 4" pipe stop into the transfer tube in the division wall ➡ remove each cartridge by the lifting bands and gently hose down ➡ remove 2" standpipe and the water in the biological stage will empty and discharge to waste ➡ hose down the entire base of the biological stage ➡ replace the 2" standpipe ➡ remove the pipe stop from the division wall – the biological stage will now fill with water ➡ switch on the main water pump and the system is back to full running operation.

<u>**Now we have a 'brand new' filtration system once again with no hidden nasties whatsoever. This can also remain to be 'brand new' forever.**</u>

Coming back to the beginning of this chapter, this system only requires the removal of 1.82 cubic metres of soil and there has to be no further excavation for access ladders or steps to access the discharge valves associated with deeper systems. If accurate costs of the true total outlay for building this system is compared to the costs of ready-made units, I think you will be very pleasantly surprised.

As mentioned earlier, this system will easily handle 3,200 UK gallons but if, say, a 6,400 UK gallon system is required then use two bottom drains and two identical filters to the one above.

- <u>Please note here, do not attempt to increase the filtration capacity by enlarging the dimensions of the chamber and the media. The dimensions of the above chamber are exact and the overall efficiency depends on several factors such as retention time in the filter *(flow rates)* and also effective flow patterns and maximum water 'disturbance'.</u>

**<u>Flow rates through the filter system</u>** – this is important, especially for the biological stage of the system. Generally the entire pond water volume should pass through the filters every two to two and a half hours. For example in a 3,200 UK gallon system described above, the flow rate through the filters should be between 1,280 to 1,600 gallons per hour.

- *Note – most water pumps give performance rates at nil head and without taking into account pipe work and fittings.*

- *'Friction loss' caused by pipe work, pipe work bore and assorted fittings can seriously reduce the output delivery of most water pumps.*

- *The actual performance of a pump can only be made by timing the delivery into a given container of known volume by stop watch or by using a purpose-made flow valve to get exact performance rates.*

- *Wherever possible use long radius bends on your feed and return pipework rather than 90 degree elbows – the long radius bends allow for a far better flow rate.*

**Water pumps** – there are many different types available on the market ranging from central heating circulator pumps, submersible pumps and surface mounted pumps. These come with various warranty periods, differing performance ratings and varied electrical consumption costs.

**Submersible water pump**

**External water pump**

Once you have calculated the volume your pump needs to deliver in one hour I suggest you purchase a unit rated at 1.5 times your actual requirements. *(For example:- If you need to pump 1,000 UK gallons per hour at no head, buy a pump rated at 1,500 UK gallons per hour.)*

- It is simple and safe to reduce the delivery of any pump by fitting a valve **after** the output *(never restrict the suction inlet)* but it is impossible to increase the maximum output of the unit should it be found to under-perform.

**Ultra-violet clarifiers** – periodically a Koi pond will experience a green water period due to a combination of algae bloom and direct sunlight. In view of this it is wise to incorporate a suitable ultra-violet clarifier into the system which will destroy the green water after passing the pond water through the unit for several days.

In a pump-fed system the U/V unit should be installed before the filter and in a gravity-fed system the U/V unit should be installed after the filter. There are several different sizes of U/V available each designed to cope with differing volumes of water in the total system. It is always a good idea to purchase a unit which can treat more water than the actual pond in question.

*Please also note once again that these units are installed purely to eradicate 'green water' – they have no effect at all in eradicating algae, blanket weed, parasites or bacteria.*

Generally all bulbs on these units have an effective life of around six months – after which new lamp/s should be fitted. There is also no need at all to switch off ultra-violet clarifiers when an anti-parasite medication has been added to the pond despite what many still profess.

**Aeration** this is also vital to both pond and biological stages of the filter in a good Koi pond system. This becomes much more important especially during summer when water temperatures are high and dissolved oxygen content is automatically reduced. Koi need a good dissolved oxygen content *(at least 6.00ppm)* in order to thrive and feed well.

**Air pump** - These are available from many distributors and retailers. They come in various outputs ranging from 25 to 200 litres of air per minute. All units are usually supplied with manifolds and fittings for simple connection to air lines and air stones.

In recent years aeration supply to the pond can be added by specially designed diffuser bottom drains mentioned earlier which supply, via a suitable air pump, a 9" diameter column of gentle diffusion of air to the pond. Other methods of adding aeration to the pond and biological stage of the filter is also by air pump and air lines feeding 2" diameter air stones or free-standing air diffusers.

**Supplementary aeration provided in mud ponds during the warm water periods by electric-powered paddles.**

**Incidentally - It is absolutely impossible to 'over-aerate' water by simply using air pumps and diffusers/air stones in a Koi pond.**

When installing air pumps it is important that they are positioned above the pond/filter water level in order to ensure that they do not flood by 'back-siphoning' of water if the pump is switched off or if a power cut takes place.

**Surface skimmers** – in ponds where leaves can be problematic from time to time, it may be wise to include a surface skimmer in the overall design in order to keep the pond surface free from floating debris. These units are designed for swimming pools and are relatively simple to install to both liner and concrete ponds. A basket set inside the skimmer catches the debris which is emptied as and when necessary.

**Removing internal basket**  **Emptying basket**

The unit is usually powered by a separate pump which returns water directly to the pond and also provides extra current. Many collectors use the pump which powers the skimmer to also power a heating system before returning water to the pond.

<u>Flowmeter</u> – when any Koi pond system is completed and ready for mains water **it is absolutely vital that filling is made via an accurate flow meter and recorded carefully for the future.** Most plumber's supply outlets have these for sale.

**Flowmeter**

Once the pond is full and water starts to exit via the overflow, the meter reading should be taken and logged for future reference.

This is vital information when accurate measures of anti-parasite medications may have to be used to the total volume of water to be treated.

<u>Pipework, valves and fittings</u> – a Koi pond uses many of these items. The pipework and fittings we use for our Koi pond should always be to 'UPVC Pressure Specification' these are designed to both retain and circulate water constantly.

**UPVC pressure pipework and fittings**

Do NOT use household drainage systems which are not intended to retain water. Instead these are only to be used to take waste water to a drain or sewer and will not survive for long in re-circulating operations.

Once again, wherever you can, try to incorporate long-radius elbows rather than ninety degree bends as this allows for greater water flow with less 'friction loss'.

Also by using larger bore return pipelines, than the fittings supplied with the pump, one gets a far better performance from the pump. For example, if the fittings on the pump are 1.5" then use 2" pipe lines by fitting 1.5" to 2" reducers in order to increase the bore.

Another point to note is that pumps, ultra-violet clarifiers and other equipment do require periodic servicing and cleaning. It is wise, therefore, to install double union ball valves **before and after each item** so these can be isolated and removed without having to cut the pipe lines at some future date.

Incidentally, when selecting the valves for your system do try to avoid 'slide' or 'knife' valves as they have proven to fail too often on too many occasions – instead try to use good quality ball valves which should last indefinitely. When your system is finally running properly, it is of vital importance that it is maintained properly and discharged regularly. This careful attention is the making of a very good Koi keeper.

**Good quality ball valves**

Before closing this chapter on Koi pond filtration, the two photographs above say it all. The one on the left shows a breeder in Junidaira village managing to get by with a very ancient above-ground 'pump-fed' filter. The other picture shows a more modern approach to the subject – or, does it?………….I'll leave this to the readers to judge.

But…………..isn't there room here for a little bit of 'middle-ground'?

- *Please note - a Koi pond incorporates many electrical items such as water pumps; air pumps; ultra-violet units and other equipment which are all in use near water.*

- *Do ensure you have a suitable earth leakage circuit breaker fitted to all electrical equipment and switch gear*

# 6. HEATING A KOI POND

Despite what many may profess, **Koi are not a true cold water species** as are Golden Orfe, Sturgeon, Goldfish and some other species of native fish that dwell in garden ponds.

*(Yes, many Koi do survive a UK winter but many more do not. <u>The ones we see very motionless and huddled together on the pond base during a cold UK winter are very unhappy indeed – please take my word for this!</u> Another myth we hear with regularity is that Koi* *'hibernate'* *– again take my word, Bears do, but Koi most certainly do not!)*

Koi bred in Japan are grown in warm, outdoor mud ponds from June until October and then harvested.

**Japanese indoor, heated Koi house used for sales and over-wintering of stocks**

They are then kept in indoor, heated glass or clear polycarbonate houses throughout the harsh winter months for protection against outdoor temperatures.

<u>All Koi imported from Japan today have rarely experienced water temperatures below 60F (15C).</u>

However we should try to give our Koi the four seasons of the year but certainly not as harsh as our outdoor UK ambient temperatures dictate. Ideal water temperature parameters are as follows:-

- **Winter** – (December to February) Minimum 50F or 9.9C

- **Spring** – (March to May) 55F (12.7C) rising to 60F (15.5C)

- **Summer** – (June to August) 64F (18C) up to 77F (25C) then slowly down to 68F (20C)

- **Autumn** – (September to November) 68F (20C) slowly down to 59F (15C)

Certainly some form of heating should be incorporated in the UK even if this is only in emergency for the odd, rare days of very low temperatures. In recent years our winters are becoming milder but I would advise an in-line electric heater to be fitted if **only as a safety measure.** If this is ever needed for a few days, it is comforting to know that heat is available.

Many enthusiasts cover and insulate their ponds and filters to minimise on heat loss which is usually by 'wind chill'. Correct temperatures can usually be achieved by adding only a small amount of heat in these instances.

**300w heaters**

**'In-Line' electric Koi pond heater**

Small systems, well insulated, can get by with two or more 300 watt aquarium heaters placed into the filter flow whilst larger insulated systems can use in-line electric 3kw to 6kw heaters working on a thermostat to achieve and maintain the desired temperature.

As to much larger systems, natural gas powered heating units and stainless-steel heat exchangers are the usual choice but, in general, our winters are now not nearly as severe as in years gone by. Koi kept in these conditions and fed as recommended in this book will come out of winter in perfect condition whereas Koi left to the UK winter elements without any form of heat usually show significant health problems in spring as water temperatures begin to rise naturally.

**This photograph shows a Japanese breeder's Koi house for his stocks to be kept from early October to late May. The ponds are kept at the required water temperatures with a simple oil-fired heater system.**

# 7. WATER

Someone said to me many years ago – *'We don't keep Koi, we just keep water'* – that is indeed the truth of the matter and it still applies today.

The subject of water is complex – and that is an understatement. Both mains water and pond water make-up varies from area to area and from pond to pond.

There are volumes upon volumes of specialist textbooks written on the many aspects of water quality – alas - one has to be a marine biologist to understand them! Furthermore, many of these scientific books do not cover the needs of Koi keepers.

For us Koi keepers, water is the single most important word in the hobby as water is the key element in all forms of fish keeping. Our water in a Koi pond is subject to constant deterioration as the Koi and other organisms are depleting the beneficial minerals. As a result, and from time to time, partial water changes will be required.

Hopefully the running operation of our pond and filters and our regular pond maintenance will keep our water parameters good for our Koi and this is where our observation and keeping skills come to the fore.

For the newcomer to the hobby a basic range of water test kits are vital, namely pH; nitrite; ammonia and dissolved oxygen.

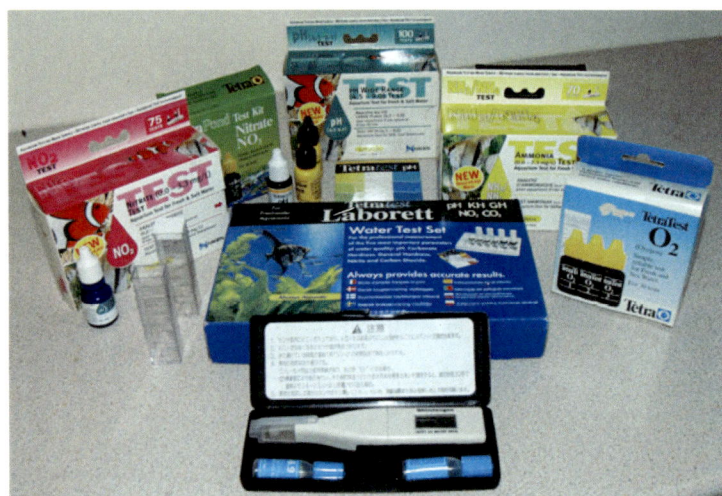

**Water test kits**

New pond systems will get severe swings in pH; nitrite and ammonia readings (*see nitrification process and 'new pond syndrome'*) but mature systems ideally need the following readings:-

### pH ideal – 7.0 to 8.0 and stable.

'pH' is an abbreviation for the 'power' or 'potential' of hydrogen content within the water. The pH scale is a man-made scale ranging from one to fourteen to determine how much the water is influenced by acids or bases.

The pH table is best understood by starting in the centre, at a neutral point, as represented by value 7.0 and moving downwards to indicate ever increasing **acidic** concentrations. As values move up from seven the chart indicates an ever increasing **alkaline** concentration to the water. Some enthusiasts consider 7.5 to 7.7 to be the ideal.

**Oyster shell used as pH buffer**

Whilst the Koi can tolerate a wide range of pH, the biological filter cannot operate at low pH below 6.5 and buffers have to be added to rectify the situation.

### Nitrite ideal – 0.0 and stable.

Nitrite is a by-product of ammonia which is present in the nitrification process. A good biological stage, fully matured, will ensure that all toxic nitrite is quickly converted by the biomass to non-toxic or 'less toxic' nitrate before being returned to the pond.

### Ammonia ideal – 0.0 and stable.

Ammonia in very minute quantities should always be present in our ponds, this is constantly given off by our Koi in urine and gill action. However the biomass in our mature biological stages should ensure that this reading cannot be detected during a standard water test. Ammonia readings can prove fatal if not attended to, and remedied, quickly and correctly.

### Dissolved Oxygen ideal – 6.0ppm and over.

This is important to both pond and biological stages of our filter system. If readings are low then dissolved oxygen content can be increased by adding extra aeration via a suitable air pump and diffusers. When one makes regular checks of pond water with the test kit it is always worthwhile to make periodic checks on our tap water for pH especially. If mains water supplies pose a problem there are companies specialising in mains water purification equipment which can generally rectify the problem. In my experience of this, a simple and cheap mains water dechlorinator unit is all that is required.

When waste water has been discharged from a system after cleaning the mechanical stage of the filter this has to be replaced with new water to top-up the system. I find the best way of doing this is by adding a small trickle of mains water into the system at all times which permanently takes the small trickle of waste water to the system overflow. By introducing this constant trickle to the pond there is no need to 'top-up' after any discharges have been made as the trickle will slowly top up the pond again.

**Whole Oyster shell, Yagenji Koi farm**

Once a new system is fully mature and our daily discharge of waste matter is attended to then our system will stabilise and water readings should be perfect.

However, in my experience, although all readings should stabilise after seven weeks or so, a system needs to be in operation for some 18 months before we can really term this as being completely 'mature'. If, for example, pH crashes for no apparent reason it can easily be returned to normal with certain special buffers that can be obtained from most aquatic outlets.

**'Hydrolit mg' pH buffer**

## Very important:-

Pond Water subjected to natural daylight, in a mature system, produces a fine coating of 'moss-like algae' on all surfaces of the pond itself.

This is absolutely vital to the health of our Koi and they can often be seen feasting on this when other forms of food are not available. This algae contains essential minerals and vitamins that cannot be replicated by ANY manufactured Koi foods.

Many enthusiasts attempt to keep their Koi inside and these indoor systems rarely allow sufficient natural light to penetrate the water. As a result, no algae forms which then results in the pigmentation of the Koi becoming weaker. The reason for this is, that by depriving our Koi of this vital algae, we also deprive them of their vital essential minerals and vitamins.

The 'colour fading' is as a direct result of the skin of the Koi actually becoming 'thinner' and thus weaker. This usually progresses into severe bacterial infections which can only be resolved by the correct choice of antibiotics and then releasing the Koi into outdoor water which has ample supplies of this essential algae. In my own experience it is almost impossible to keep Koi healthy for any long periods of time without vital daylight.

A typical Japanese Koi breeder's indoor ponds which are used from October until late May.

**This demonstrate the vital importance of daylight in the keeping of Nishikigoi.**

## Water Hardness/Softness (KH/GH)

This may sometimes need to be checked in our pond water which contains many minerals and other compounds that cannot be detected by the human eye. These minerals are of great importance to both the internal system of the Koi, the alkalinity and ultimately, the pH of the pond water. To simplify – water hardness is linked to alkaline reserve and this alkaline reserve is the invisible strength behind a desirable and stable pH reading.

Calcium, calcium carbonate and magnesium are all at the core of the term 'water hardness' and, although other minerals such as sodium and potassium do not contribute in a major way to hardness, these are important minerals which are valuable to our Koi.

In general, water hardness/softness is classified as follows:-

- 50mg/litre – soft water
- 50 to 150mg/litre – medium hard water
- 150 to 300mg/litre – general hard water or mineral water
- Over 300mg/litre – hard water

This should show the close links between pH, alkalinity and water hardness/softness.

Many experienced Koi enthusiasts are aware that mud pond water in Japan is soft and that it also produces excellent results in the growing season. After the harvest the Koi are kept in indoor concrete systems which produce water of medium hardness.

If the pursuit of soft water in concrete filtered ponds is strived for, this can, from time to time, result in a pH crash where good water changes, calcium carbonate or oyster shell can soon rectify the matter. A constant trickle of new water can also keep this problem under control,

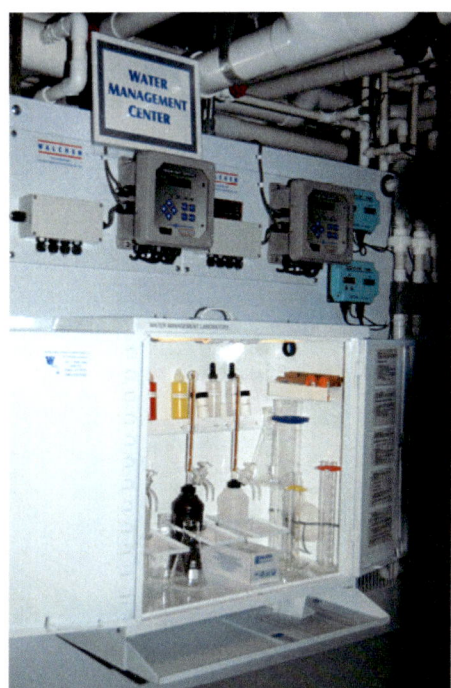

**Left** – constant monitoring of water parameters by expensive high-tech digital readout.

As mentioned earlier, no matter how good our pond water conditions are, they are also in a constant state of decay all of the time.

The better our systems are and the better our maintenance is in managing the system, this 'constant decay' should be kept under control for longer time periods.

- <u>Again, from time to time, water changes can be of great benefit to the overall excellence of the water which is the vital life-blood of our Koi.</u>

<u>Once again</u> – **'We do not keep Koi – we just keep water'!**

# 8. FEEDING OUR KOI

Here the reader has the choice of literally hundreds of different Koi foods on the shelves of many aquatic outlets everywhere – and - most profess to be 'the very best on the market'!

For the newcomer to the hobby it may be prudent to make a few enquiries with other Koi keepers as to the brand they find the best for their Koi in order to try and get some feedback. Generally my own Koi are fed 'Hikari Wheatgerm' pellets all year round, this Koi food is made in Japan and imported to the UK.

Koi are omnivorous – they will eat just about anything offered – prawns; oranges; cereals etc. etc. but this does not mean it is all good for them. Most keepers I know, including myself, use Koi pellets at all times supplemented in summer with a few treats such as prawns – *(best fed uncooked and liquidised, shell and all)*, fruits and a whole lettuce from time to time.

Good feeding regimes for our Koi are governed by water temperatures – the warmer the water, the more food they will take and the cooler the temperatures the less food they will take.

**Left** - No expensive fancy packages here for the Koi breeders of Yamakoshi. Instead just basic Koi pellets in 25 kilo paper sacks. These are delivered on request by local suppliers.

- This is the very same food fed exclusively to **ALL** grades of Koi from general grade to world class that are later shipped all around the world.

This shot opposite was taken at the Marusho Koi farm in Mushigame village. The Koi being fed are his tosai (Koi born last June) – they are kept at water temperatures around 23C and are fed four times daily.

By the following June when they are 12 months old they can measure 20cms and over.

<u>If we maintain water temperatures as recommended in this book earlier then feeding should be as follows:-</u>

- **<u>Winter</u>** – <u>December to February</u>.

At this time of the year it is not really necessary to feed at all and you should often see your Koi at this time grazing on the essential fine moss-like algae growing on the pond walls and base.

However, if you do decide to feed, keep this to one feed a day with soft, pre-soaked Koi pellets preferably in the morning. However if you decide not to feed during this period your Koi will come to no harm at all.

Also if female Koi are fed at this time of the year, much of the food taken in is usually only converted to make more eggs as opposed to making any body growth or volume as such. This could possibly result in egg compaction in the following spring which generally can lead to very complex and expert surgery.

- **<u>Spring</u>** – <u>March to May</u>.

Again use pre-soaked pellets and feed sparingly morning and evening. One should begin to see visible signs of some growth by the end of May.

- **<u>Summer</u>** – <u>June to August</u>.

During this period the feeding can be as often as the Koi demand. You cannot over-feed your Koi as they will only take what they need at any given time. However, you can over-feed your pond and filter – do make sure all food is eaten and none is left to decay. Now is the time to increase currents in the pond if possible to give more exercise to the Koi. A whole lettuce thrown on the pond at this time of the year brings a good supplement to their diet.

- **<u>Autumn</u>** – <u>September to November</u>.

Feeding can be liberal during the first part of September using almost the same quantity of summer feeds but steadily reducing the amount fed each week towards the end of the month. By mid-October temperatures should be around 62F (17C) when only pre-soaked pellets should be used. Reduce the amount fed to one morning feed per day during the whole of November.

As to the amounts of food to feed, this depends on the number of Koi and the size of Koi to be fed and usually the day to day experience of the keeper comes to the fore here. Generally the pellets should all be taken within ten minutes or so.

In summer when both water temperatures and feeding rates are at their highest you may notice a slight fading of both red and black pigmentation on your Koi and this is quite normal. Pigmentation and lustre returns to its peak again during winter when water temperatures are lower.

# 9. CARING

From time to time our Koi may be infected by certain water-borne parasites which need prompt and accurate eradication methods in order to prevent secondary bacterial damage as a direct result of these prime parasites. Just about every other form of life suffers with parasitic infections – trees; plants; humans; birds; animals etc. etc. – in this respect, our Koi are no different.

Parasites and their un-hatched eggs, which will hatch in the pond, can be introduced to a Koi pond by frogs, newts and bird droppings as well as from new Koi purchases and water plants.

However the parasites that can and do infect our Koi generally cannot be seen with the naked eye. They live and reproduce mainly in the delicate mucus membrane which protects the Koi or in the fragile gill filaments of the Koi themselves. These microscopic parasites are most generally gill flukes; skin flukes; white spot; epistylis; trichodina; costia; chilodonella plus visible parasites such as anchor worm and argulus.

These parasites can reproduce very quickly depending on water temperature. They can reproduce at an alarming rate and become a serious problem if not detected early and the correct steps are taken to eradicate the particular parasite in question.

Unfortunately there is no single chemical or remedy that will eradicate all these parasites. Instead we have to use different chemicals or remedies in specific dosage rates in order to successfully eradicate the different species present.

In view of this we must come from a scientific approach in order to determine the actual parasite in question. This can only be carried out by taking a mucus sample from the body or the gills and inspecting it under a microscope.

**It is pointless and completely useless simply trying to 'guess' which particular parasite is present.**

Generally, in a Koi pond, if one Koi is suffering with a particular parasite we can assume that all the Koi are infected, which means that the total pond system has to be treated.

There are some amongst us who profess -

'You'll never catch **ME** putting chemicals in **MY** pond'

- but, from my experiences, <u>if parasites are present they need eradicating as quickly as is possible before far more serious secondary bacterial damages arise.</u>

There is no doubt in my mind that Koi are far happier and healthier *without* parasites!

Some symptoms of a parasitic problem in our Koi are usually very similar to those where poor water quality is the culprit.

Tell-tale signs are – 'flashing against the walls or base of the pond; jumping out of the water; no interest in feeding; hovering at the water surface and breathing rapidly' – in view of this it is best to first check that all our water quality parameters are satisfactory.

Most experienced Koi keepers own microscopes and know how to use them but for the newcomer this may not be the case.

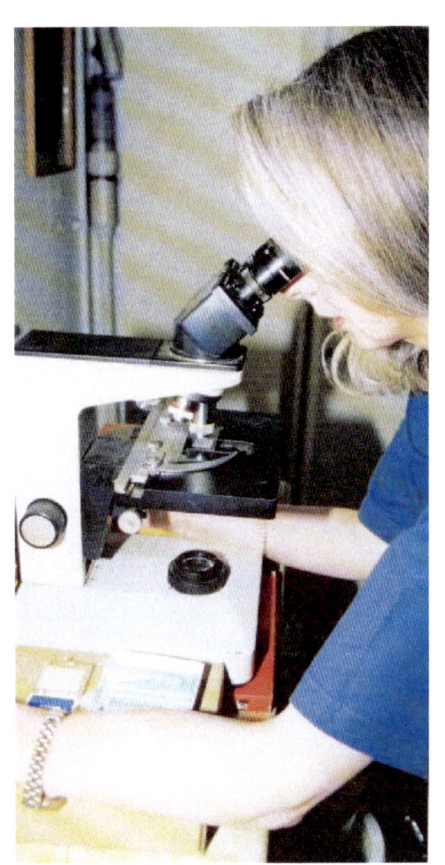

### Using a microscope

However, most reputable Koi dealers will offer a service whereby an enthusiast can bring a Koi for an inspection. The dealer will then take a sample of mucus and check it under a microscope and then determine the particular parasite in question that is causing the problem.

*This is when it becomes **vital** to know the **exact** volume of water held in the system as all anti-parasite remedies are calculated specifically to the water volume of the pond system in question.*

When adding anti-parasite remedies to a Koi pond it is important that the filter is running as normal as parasites and eggs can be re-circulated throughout the entire system. In general, most of these medications do have a temporary adverse effect on the biomass within the filter but a good, mature filter will easily handle this and recover to full operation very quickly without any harm to the Koi at all.

It is also interesting to note that some of the medications and dosage rates still effective today in eradicating some species of parasites were first experimented with, and used, by the early fish farmers many years ago. Formalin, malachite green and potassium permanganate all spring to mind here. The precise dosage rates specified later in this chapter work on a 'strength to water volume' principle whereby the medication destroys the particular parasite in question without harming the Koi themselves. There are also many effective 'short-term' baths for these medications which require much stronger dosage rates but for a significantly shorter time period.

Before we continue on to specific dosages perhaps it is better to cover weights and measures first:-

**One ton of water weighs 1,000 kilograms and equals one cubic metre**
**= 1,000 litres**
**= 1,000,000 millilitres**
**= 220 Imperial gallons**
**= 264 US gallons**

**One litre of water weighs 1 kilogram = 1,000 grams.**

**If calculating UK tons – example 4,500 gallons divide by 220 = 20.45 tons.**

**If calculating USA tons – example 4,500 gallons divide by 264 = 17.04 tons.**

# Anti-parasite medications and dosage rates

- **<u>Please note, these dosages are specifically for Koi and carp – do not use if other species of fish are present. When handling these chemicals use protective rubber gloves and a face mask.</u>**

There are many dozens of so-called remedies on the market said to cure both parasitic and bacterial disorders and one can see these on display in brightly coloured packaging at many outlets. In all my years of being involved in Nishikigoi I have yet to find a single one to be effective despite the outrageous claims and expensive advertising made.

## 1. <u>White Spot, Chilodonella and Epistylis (microscopic)</u>

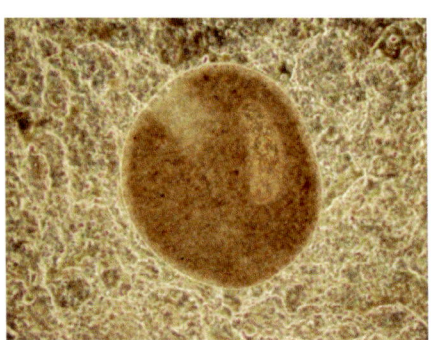 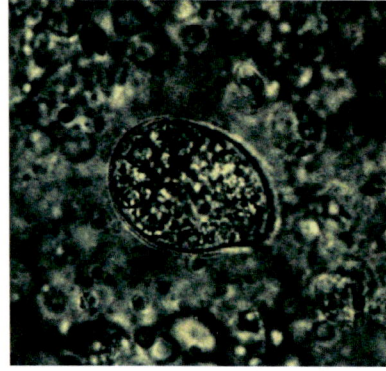 

**White Spot (high mag.)**   **Chilodonella (high mag.)**   **Epistylis (high mag.)**

Use a combination of zinc-free malachite green crystals at the rate of 0.25 grams per ton of water plus a 36% solution of 'Analar' grade formalin at the rate of 15mls per ton of water.

*<u>Do not use this medication if pond water temperatures are below 50F . Also do not use formalin if the pond water has a salt content over 2.5kilos per ton.</u>*

Example – In a 3,200 gallon pond (14.52 tons) use 3.63 grams malachite green plus 217mls. formalin.

Method – dissolve the malachite green crystals in a bucket of warm water and stir thoroughly, then add the formalin and stir. Pour directly into the pond around the perimeter. Water turns dark green and clears after 1 to 2 days.

## 2. <u>Gill Flukes and Skin Flukes (microscopic)</u>

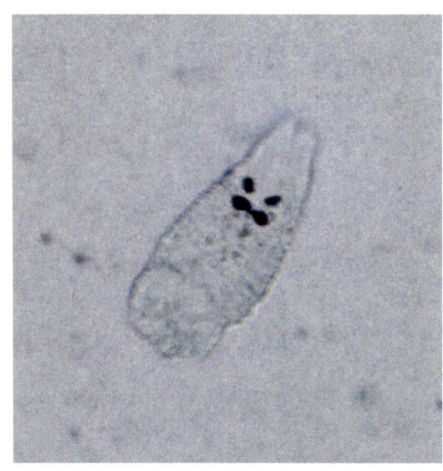 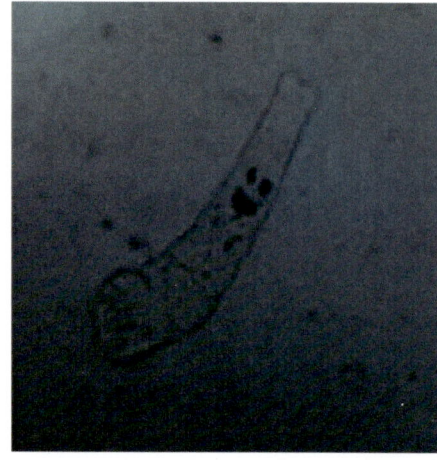

**Gill fluke (Dactylogyrus)**

Very high maginification

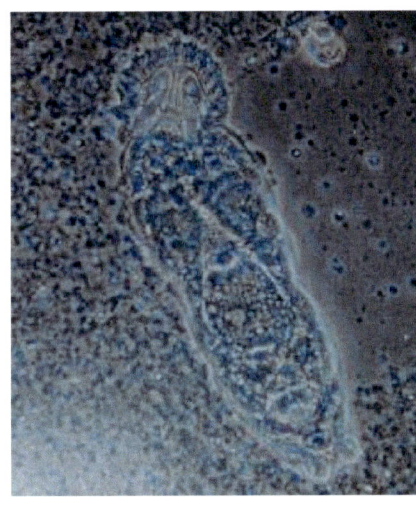
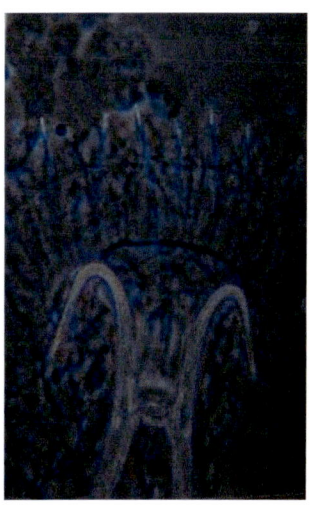

**Skin fluke (Gyrodactylus)**

Very high magnification

Use 'Flubenol' *(a fine, white powder)* available from most veterinarians, at the rate of 2.5grams per ton of water. This is commonly used to 'de-worm' both domestic pets and farm animals.

Example - in a 3,200 gallon pond (14.52 tons) use 36.36grams of Flubenol, the powder must be dissolved thoroughly in warm water before adding to pond.

Method – mix 'Flubenol' in a bucket of warm water and stir thoroughly, alternatively shake it well with water in a strong polythene bag – this product does not readily dissolve in water. Pour into the pond around the perimeter. Water turns cloudy and clears after 1 to 2 days.

### 3. Trichodina and Costia (microscopic)

**Trichodina**          **Costia**

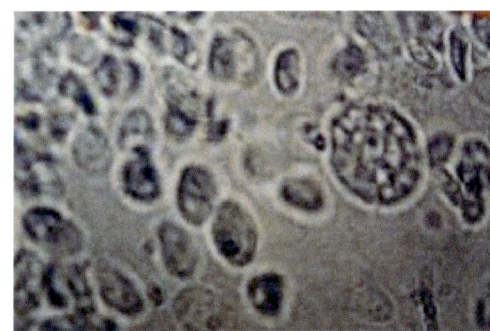

(Both of the above shots are taken at **very** high magnification)

Use potassium permanganate 'Analar grade' powder at the rate of 1.5 grams per ton of water.

Example - in a 3,200 gallon pond (14.52 tons) use 21.7grams of potassium permanganate.

Method – dissolve the potassium permanganate crystals in a bucket of warm water by stirring thoroughly and leave to stand for 30 minutes, then stir thoroughly again. Pour into the pond around the perimeter. Water turns purple and later becomes brown, it then clears after 2 to 3 days. Note:- On very rare occasions when an infestation of either of these two parasites is present in very high numbers and the pond treatment does not eradicate them all successfully, one can use a potassium permanganate bath for the Koi at the rate of 10 grams per ton of water for 90 minutes duration together with good aeration.

## 4. Anchor Worm (Lernea)

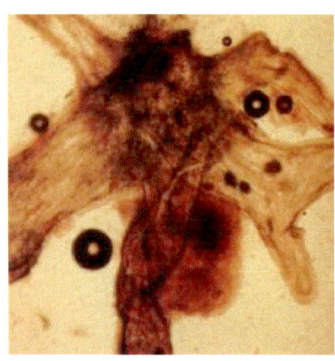

**Anchor Worm.**

**(Left)** - This is a high magnification of the head part of the parasite, the 'anchors' can be seen clearly here. The actual tail of the parasite can be seen **(right)** with the naked eye and looks like a white thread of cotton protruding out from under a scale.

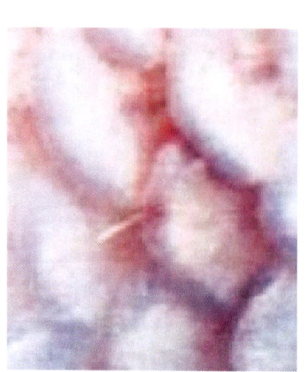

Use 'Dimilin' powder at the rate of 1 gram per ton of water.

Example - in a 3,200 gallon pond (14.52 tons) use 14.52grams of Dimilin.

Method – add Dimilin to a bucket of warm water, stir thoroughly. Pour into the pond around the perimeter. Water turns cloudy and clears after 1 to 2 days. It can be difficult to locate this product today.

Note – Dimilin does not kill the anchor worm, instead it **sterilises** the adult parasite so that any new eggs produced *after* the treatment will not hatch. Also the dead anchor worm will still be attached to the Koi. These parasites need to be removed which means anaesthetic has to be used and the entire anchor worm has to be carefully removed by tweezers. This is a job for the professional handler.

## 5. Fish Louse (Argulus) & Leeches

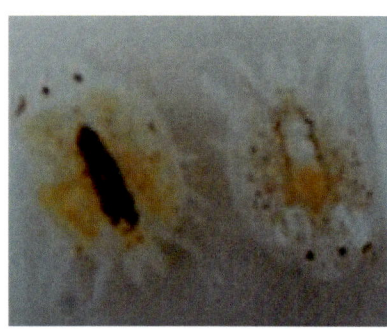

**Argulus**

Both of these are also visible by the naked eye and are more commonly seen in ponds containing water plants. Use 'Masoten' or 'Dipterex' powder at the rate of 1.0 grams per ton of water. These products are organophosphates and, as such, are deemed illegal to use in our eco-system. Location of these products can be difficult today – but, not impossible.

Example in a 3,200 gallon pond (14.52 tons) use 14.52grams of Masoten.

Method – dissolve Masoten powder in a bucket of warm water and mix thoroughly. Pour directly into the pond around the perimeter. Water turns cloudy and clears after several hours. Generally speaking, if these anti-parasite pond medications are applied correctly they will eradicate the parasite in question completely but will have no effect on any un-hatched eggs which are naturally protected. To make sure that a medication has been totally successful a further mucus sample should be checked by microscope after 3 days of adding the initial medication.

**NOTE – All these chemicals mentioned can be extremely dangerous. Store in a cool, dry area, always wear rubber gloves and a breathing mask when handling. Keep out of reach of children and pets.**

## Bacterial problems – lesions and ulcerations.

These can be the result of many causes, examples such as:-

- Secondary infection from a prime parasite.

- Self-inflicted damage from a Koi jumping, scratching or spawning.

- Inexperienced netting or handling techniques.

- Damage from a bird or other predator – very rare in a good Koi pond.

Whatever the reason, the Koi needs urgent attention as these lesions will only deteriorate unless they are taken care of quickly. <u>This usually means the Koi has to be anaesthetised and the correct antibiotic injection administered. This is a task for a professional. In view of this it is recommended you should contact a local Koi dealer for assistance should any of these problems arise.</u>

**Ulcer**

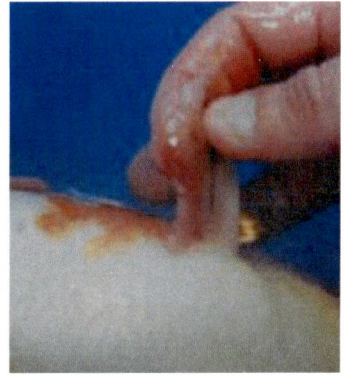
**Fin damage**

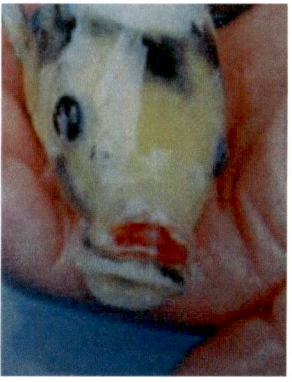
**Mouth damage**

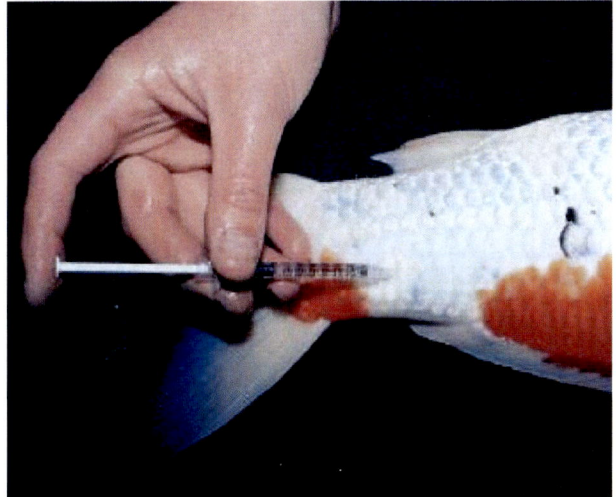
**Technique showing point of injection**

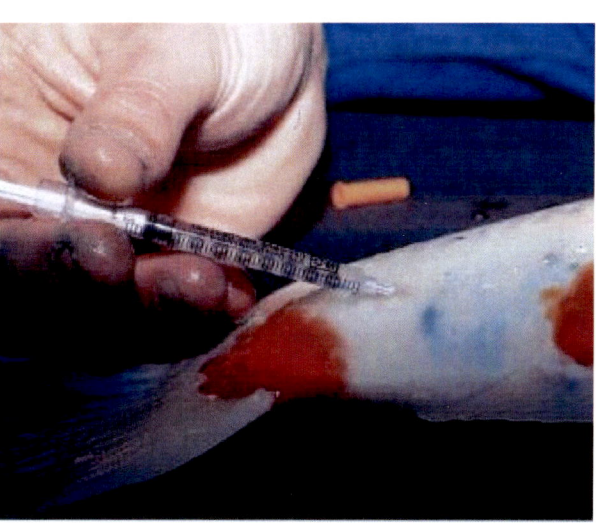
**Correct angle of injection**

The earlier a potential problem is detected the easier it is to effect a cure. A good time to visually inspect your Koi is when they are feeding. If you see one or more Koi showing no interest in food this could be a sign that something is amiss and steps have to be taken to determine the problem in order to rectify the situation.

Prior to the vast numbers of heated ponds we see nowadays, many of us, in the early days, had to cope annually with a problem we all came to know as 'spring sickness'. This was detected as some Koi started to break out with ulcerations when water temperatures slowly increased after a long, cold winter. This was directly due to aeromonas infection at a time when our Koi were weak due to low water temperatures and a filter not as biologically mature as it is in warm water periods. The 'aeromonas' on the other hand were not affected at all by this having spent winter consuming food, reproducing and consolidating.

Even in heated systems outbreaks of aeromonas can cause significant problems and the resulting lesions and infections are a very real threat.

It should be noted here that most of the antibiotics and chemicals mentioned above are only available through veterinarians and some others through specialist Koi outlets. These remedies are used by most Koi professionals and experienced Koi enthusiasts but are not generally sold over the counter. It is wise to have these on hand should the need arise.

However, merely by owning effective supplies of injectible antibiotics such as 'Baytril 10%'; 'Azactam'; 'Amikacin' and 'Gentamycin' etc. we still do not know which particular antibiotic or antibiotics are specifically effective in producing a cure for the bacterial problem we may be faced with. The only accurate way this can be determined is by contacting your veterinarian who may be able to take a swab of the infected area and send it away for laboratory analysis.

After a few days the report will come back and list which particular antibiotics are determined as 'gram positive' *(effective)* in the eradication of these particular types of bacteria and will effect good healing.

During the period where one is awaiting results, the area of damage can be brought under some control by painting a good topical dressing on the area of damage. A good choice here is a UK made product known as 'iosal'.

**I must also point out here that there are no antibiotics produced specifically for Koi.**

- The antibiotics commonly used, and found to be effective in the treatment of our Koi, are made for animals or humans. <u>As to injection dosage rates, this also has not been arrived at by any scientific means at all and these can vary from keeper to keeper.</u> If you need further assistance on these matters I suggest you contact your local Koi dealer who should be able to help with some accurate advice from experience.

In view of the minute amounts of anti-parasite chemicals required and covered earlier, I strongly suggest the purchase of an accurate gram balance which weighs to 0.1 gram intervals. It would also be prudent to own an accurate plastic liquid measuring cylinder and a plastic funnel.

### Gram balance accurate to 0.1 gram

Finally, on this subject, there are rare occasions when both water quality checks are perfect and mucus scrapes reveal that no parasites are present and yet the Koi are obviously unhappy.

This generally indicates that there is another problem within the system itself.

More often than not this is due to an excessive build-up of general bacteria that is irritating the Koi and causing them to scratch.

In these situations we can use 'Chloramine T' to reduce the overall bacteria count. Chloramine T is an 'aquatic bleach' which acts as a disinfectant to treat the system in question – usually with perfect results. However, dosage rates of this product vary with both hard and soft water as well as pH readings. It is wise to consult a professional in order to calculate the amount required for your pond water qualities and water volume.

I also feel I should briefly mention, in this chapter, two other non-parasitic or bacterial problems that can sometimes usually affect high quality Koi more so than general grade Koi.

- The first is known as **'shimi'** *(freckle)* which is seen by one or two random tiny small black spots appearing quite suddenly on the red (beni) scales of Kohaku varieties mainly. This can de-value a Koi significantly and many can be removed surgically by an expert.

- The second problem here is that of **'hikui'** which is a form of skin cancer that only affects the red (beni) pigment of Go-Sanke varieties. This appears as a small area of 'light yellow-orange' in the form of a small, 'slightly raised area' on the body, it can be very gently removed by scraping this away but it generally returns soon afterwards.

Neither of these problems transmit from Koi to Koi and occurrence is not really common but, to date, no real cure has been found nor the reasons for these manifestations in the first place. The Koi shows no signs of sickness and simply continues to behave as normal.

The above text in this chapter should provide a wealth of information on parasitic and bacterial disorders that can affect our Koi from time to time. The treatments and remedies are also as specific and up to date as is currently possible.

The Japanese breeders also experience their Koi suffering with parasitic disorders especially after their stocks have been harvested from the mud ponds. However, the breeders themselves rarely own or have access to a microscope. Many have also admitted to me that even if they did own one, they would not be able to identify the particular parasite seen. Instead, if they detect their stocks are, and I quote – **'Not Well'** – they simply contact their local village office and request assistance.

Soon afterwards a member of the village office staff will visit the farm together with all the necessary equipment and then take random mucus samples from all ponds. After this he inspects the samples by microscope and relates his findings to the breeder. He will then take details as to the water volumes of each system that requires treatment. After this he will return to his laboratory and measure out exactly the type and amount of chemicals required. Later he returns to the breeder and doses his systems accordingly and the offending parasite is eradicated – furthermore, the total service is free from charge.

Unfortunately most Koi keepers do not have this luxury to hand and so we must take on the task ourselves or, alternatively, employ our local Koi dealer to assist. Once again, the earlier a problem is detected, the easier it is to resolve.

# 10. MISCELLANY

## a. HANDLING

From time to time, we all have to handle our Koi whether it is to inspect one for a suspected damage or simply to take a photograph or a measurement of the Koi in a bowl. Perhaps a Koi needs to be transported to a show or taken to a Koi dealer for mucus inspection etc.

### Correct method of netting a Koi

Great care should be taken whilst netting a Koi and the operation should be carried out slowly to avoid damaging the Koi or dislodging any scales.

There are Koi nets and Koi handling nets on the market specifically made for this purpose and the Koi net has a shallow, saucer-shaped net as opposed to the angler's deep landing net.

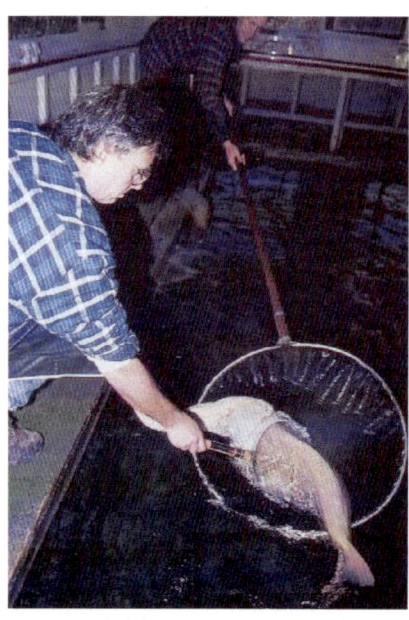

It is generally a two man operation, one to coax the Koi through the water in the net *(never lift a Koi out of the water in the Koi net)* and another to lift the Koi in a handling net and then place it into a nearby bowl of water. If a Koi handling net is not available a plastic Koi bag will do equally as well.

### Correct method of lifting a Koi

If the Koi has to travel some distance, then boxes, bags and rubber bands will be needed together with pure oxygen to inflate the bag. This may require your local dealer to assist you here.

When introducing new Koi to your pond it is necessary to float the Koi on the pond inside the sealed plastic bag it was transported in. Usually after 10 minutes to 20 minutes of floating on the pond it will ensure that the water temperatures in both bag and pond will have equalised. Then open the bag and add small quantities of pond water to the bag before gently releasing the Koi into the pond. It is also better to dispose of the water in which the Koi has travelled.

Newly-introduced Koi can sometimes have difficulty in adjusting to new water quality and some tend to try and escape by jumping out and this is usually where 'new water' is entering the pond *(waterfalls or return pipes from filters etc.)* In view of this it is best to protect these areas for the first few days until the new Koi has fully adjusted to the water quality in the pond.

## b. BREEDING YOUR KOI

Whilst it is not difficult to spawn your Koi it is not recommended unless you have ample time to spare as rearing the fry and maintaining your water quality is extremely time-consuming.

It is better not to try to spawn the Koi in your main pond as the spawning activities can cause severe body damage. Instead buy or borrow a large show pond or similar, just as long as the pond has soft sides in order to prevent the Koi damaging themselves during the frenzied spawning process.

July is a good time of the year to try this when water temperatures are warm. After the portable pond is filled with a mixture of both pond and tap water, add good aeration and a suitable de-chlorinator if necessary. As to spawning media, brushes can be purchased at your local Koi outlet or you can use larch branches freshly cut from the tree – these should be anchored firmly all along the base and walls of the pond.

As to the parent Koi themselves, try to use one mature female around 4 years old or more and three males around 3 years old. You will need someone with experience here to check sexes and also if the males are producing the necessary milt before they are used in the spawning.

Generally, if the parent Koi are introduced to the spawning pond in the late afternoon they can be induced into spawning by the following morning or the morning after by spraying very cold tap water or adding ice cubes onto the surface of the pond as soon as they have been introduced. This quickly reduces the pond temperature and acts as a 'trigger' to start off the spawning process.

The spawning usually starts very early in the morning and can last for three hours or more. It is important to closely watch the parent Koi here as some will start to eat the eggs after a while – any doing this should be removed. When spawning is complete and the eggs are deposited on the spawning media all parent Koi can now be removed.

**Koi eggs laid on artificial spawning grass (kinran)**

After this it is wise to rinse the eggs in a mild malachite green solution of 0.25grams to 2 tons of water by adding this to the pond and to ensure that the aeration continues at all times.

The **easy part** is now over!

Within three to six days, depending on water temperature, the eggs will hatch and the fry will cling vertically to the walls of the pond or the spawning media for up to one day. During this period they are ingesting their yolk sacs and inflating their swim bladders.

Soon afterwards they will swim horizontally and will then immediately need ample and endless supplies of infusoria or brine shrimp to feed upon.

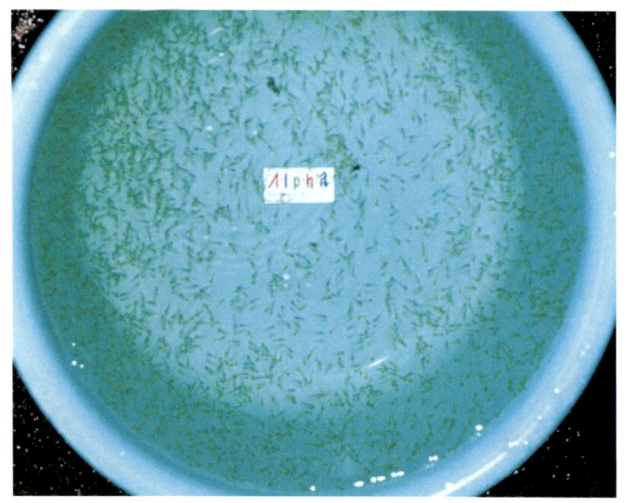

### 'Free-swimming' Koi fry

After this it is all a matter of supplying as much food as is possible without allowing the water quality to fail. This means monitoring pH; nitrite and ammonia and compensating for any poor readings by water changes. It also means having available continuous and ample supplies of live and powdered food for the significant number of fry that can be hatched from a single spawning – a mature female Koi can produce more than 250,000 eggs!

The skill in breeding Koi is not the actual spawning process itself but the rearing of the young together with the water quality parameters that require constant monitoring and attention. This is only recommended if one has sufficient time on their hands.

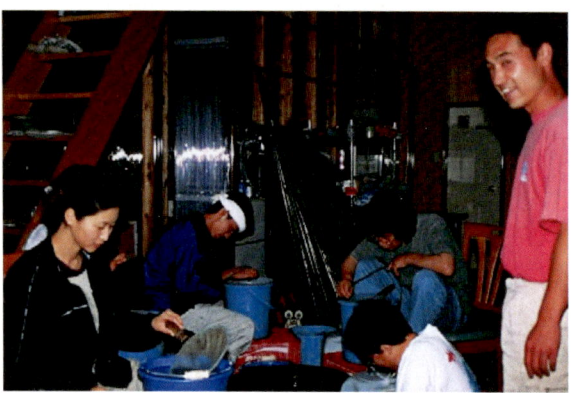

**Midnight culling of free-swimming fry at the Yamamatsu Koi farm in Mushigame village selecting 14 day old fry**

If you do require further information on the fascinating subject of breeding and rearing Koi, there are two very professional and well-established Koi farms in the UK who may be able to offer some extremely valuable assistance.

Maurice Cox at www.koi-uk.co.uk
Mark Davis at www.cuttlebrookkoifarm.co.uk

### c. BLANKET WEED

Whilst it is of paramount importance that our pond walls and base need coating with the short, fine, moss-like algae mentioned earlier, this does not include the long string algae known more commonly as 'blanket weed'.

As mentioned in the 'Filter Section' earlier, water containing non-toxic 'nitrates' is returned to the pond after the nitrification process has been completed and this can sometimes help to produce blanket weed.

Some ponds never experience blanket weed at all but many others do and this can prove to be very frustrating. Blanket weed grows at an alarming rate and can choke the bottom drains which results in filter starvation. Despite laborious and regular removal of the blanket weed manually it still continues to reproduce.

Fortunately there are several remedies available on the market to destroy blanket weed ranging from powder and liquid additives to special filter units.

If you are unfortunate enough to be faced with this problem consult your local dealer for details of the product that will suit your own water make-up in your area as this can vary.

## d. THE USE OF SALT IN A KOI POND

There are many who advocate that salt should always be used in a Koi pond as it really has antiseptic properties. However it is not recommended to use anti-parasite medications if salt is present in the pond water. In view of this, salt should only be used for a specific purpose and not as a permanent remedy.

The salt one should use for pond treatment is cooking salt which is free from the additives that table salt contains to make it flow more freely. Once salt is added to a pond it remains permanently in solution and can only be removed by adding new water in order to reduce its strength very gradually. For those with unheated ponds salt can be useful as an antiseptic for the Koi during the winter months only at the rate of 3 kilos per ton of water.

Example – in a 2,500 gallon (11.36 tons) system use 34 kilos of salt.

**Salinometer**

This can be added to the water by hand without mixing, it will completely dissolve after a short period of time. There are purpose-made salinity meters available to accurately measure the salt content in water.

*A short term salt bath at 1 kilo to 11 UK gallons of water can be useful to reduce over-production of gill mucus which can result in congestion. The duration of this bath should be 8 to 12 minutes and can be repeated daily.*

**Finally, despite what many may profess, cooking salt does <u>not</u> destroy any parasites within the system.**

## e. SHOWING YOUR KOI

Most Koi keepers come into the hobby initially with no interest at all in entering Koi shows but, after a few years, some become more involved with the hobby as their keeping and appreciation skills become better. As a result some enthusiasts do take part in local shows and ultimately may then progress to take part in larger shows. In recent years the vast majority of Koi shows staged have been held 'English-style' whereby entrants have one or more show ponds in which to enter their Koi and these are shown separate to other entrants who each have their own show ponds at the show. This method of separating all entries is to ensure there is no transmission of diseases between Koi from different entrants. In years gone by most shows were staged 'Japanese-style' whereby Koi from different entrants were entered together within variety and size classifications in the same pond.

Scenes at Japanese Koi shows

If you are considering entering your Koi to a show and you have reserved your show pond with the show officials, preparation steps should be as follows:-

- Turn off any heating to your pond at least seven days before the show – this should ensure show pond water and transportation water is roughly the same temperature.

- Stop all feeding to your Koi at least seven days before the show – this should ensure that your Koi do not pollute their show pond water during the show.

- Borrow an oxygen bottle with the regulator valve and ensure you have a supply of 'double-strength' polythene Koi bags, rubber bands and Koi cartons to transport your Koi in.

- When packing your Koi ensure there is sufficient water in the bag to cover all the Koi and that the dorsal fin is submerged.

- When loading the cartons into the car make sure they are placed across the boot of the car with the nose and tail pointing to the doors just in case there is any heavy braking – this ensures that the Koi will not damage their noses or tails in travel.

- For your return journey, oxygen is usually freely available at the show.

## f. WATER ADDITIVES

As mentioned earlier, Koi in Japan spend the summer months in mud ponds which are man-made and excavated from the clay mountainsides in the area. The Japanese breeders claim that the mineral properties of the clay together with low stocking rates and good feeding regimes all combine to make significant improvements to the skin of the Koi.

For many years now we have used 'Refresh Powder' which is manufactured in Japan and is made up from 'Montmorillionite Clay' together with added minerals as a conditioner for pond water to try in some way to replicate the actual conditions present in the mud ponds.

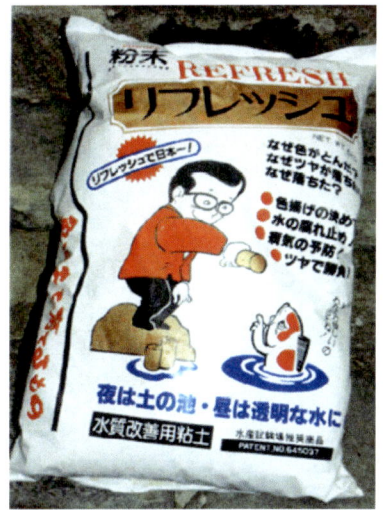

### 'Refresh'

Used correctly, this product has a real effect in improving the skin quality of the Koi by absorption and also is beneficial to the overall pond water quality.

Initial dosage is 250grams 'Refresh' to four tons (880 UK gallons) of pond water; this should be measured out and placed into a large bowl. Pond water is then added and mixed thoroughly by hand to ensure all lumps have been removed when it then takes on a similar thickness to emulsion paint. This is then added to the pond water which becomes very muddy for some three days or so before clarity returns. Top-up dosages should be carried out at monthly intervals after the total water discharged has been estimated. For example, if 1,760 gallons has been discharged to waste in any given month then 500grams of Refresh should be added accordingly.

## g. QUARANTINE

Koi do not need to be legally quarantined before they enter the country of import but all shipments of Koi into the UK have to be accompanied by a current health certificate signed by a veterinarian who has inspected them in the country exporting them. Many importers of Koi have their own quarantine procedures which they use for new arrivals before they put them on sale. This is usually checking by microscope that no parasites are present and that any physical damages caused in transit have been treated and healed. If parasites are present – and this is common – then the appropriate anti-parasite chemicals are used to eradicate them. In recent years there have been instances of several serious viral outbreaks – notably SVC (Spring Viraemia of Carp) and KHV (Koi Herpes Virus) and subsequent significant Koi losses which have recently sent shock waves around the industry.

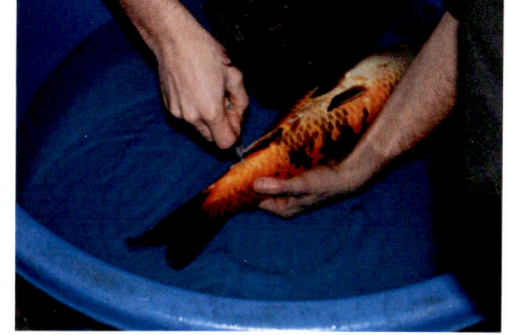

**Blood sampling for KHV test**

As a result, many Koi keepers now have their own quarantine systems and procedures which are used for any new purchases before they are allowed to join their main collection.

In my own opinion, good quarantine systems are a wise choice – always providing they are exposed to ample daylight and are producing the vital moss-like algae on the walls and base of the pond. Alas, many quarantine systems I have seen lack natural daylight and only produce average water quality which is not conducive to the health of any new arrivals that are probably weak after travel.

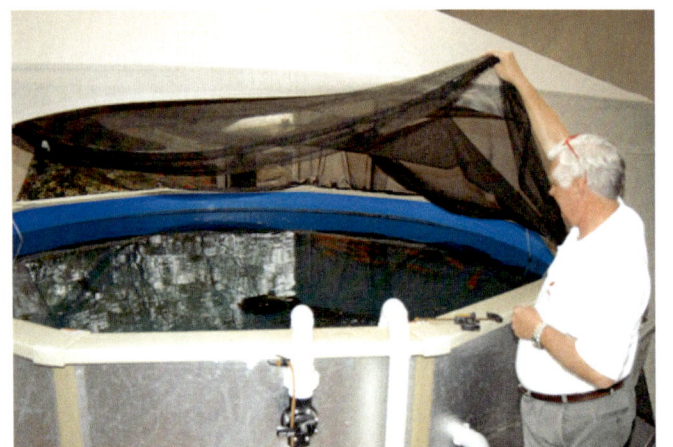

## Purpose made quarantine system

There is no doubt that care should be taken when buying any new Koi. One should check that the Koi one is thinking of buying is in perfect condition – no torn fins and no physical lesions. It should also swim well, breathe normally and take food if offered. The general condition of all the Koi at the particular outlet must be checked visually first before even thinking of making a purchase.

If you are inexperienced in buying Koi, it is always good if a more experienced keeper can accompany you on any visits where purchases may be made.

Most professional Koi outlets trade on their reputations through past business dealings and it would be against their better interests to sell any Koi with a suspected problem or one in poor health.

If you buy your Koi with care there should be no reason why it cannot join your main collection immediately but if you have adequate quarantine facilities then there is no harm in placing it in quarantine for a period of time. Ultimately the decision on 'quarantine' vs. 'no quarantine' rests with the individual!

**This superb oil painting was presented to me in 1988 by the Watanabe family in Budokubo village. It depicts the actual parents used to produce the original 'JINBEI' Sanke bloodline. The male parent is at the top of the painting.**

This is a replica of a Japanese sculpture, famous throughout Japan and simply known as 'Boy with Carp'.

Woodblock of a Yamakoshi scene

I have had this original work since 1982 when it was presented to me by the late Hiroshi Kawakami of the Urakawa Koi farm in Uragara village. The Koi here are made from porcelain and depict the parents used to produce the original 'Torazo' line of Taisho Sanke. The male Koi is on top. I doubt if Tsuyoshi, his son, has ever seen this before.

# 11. MY MENTORS

I could not have completed this book without a little self-indulgence and in the hope that some readers of this book out there would, in the future, take a true journey of a lifetime to the very part of the world where the first-ever Nishikigoi were produced. I really hope that this text below will tempt you.

I have honestly forgotten just how many visits I have made to Japan since my very first time in 1977 to try, and try, to learn the real truth about Nishikigoi. In those days it was just about impossible to even attempt to break into the minds of the real Nishikigoi breeders without first having to employ expensive guides and agents. Back then the geography of the main producing area made travel very difficult – even the guides got lost. Add to that the language barrier and several new customs to adopt, it quickly became a real uphill and frustrating battle for me - the only foreigner in town in those days!

Back then it was not only the 19 hour long-haul air journey to Tokyo's Narita airport. There were also train and car journeys to get from the airport to Nagaoka City, this added a further 11 hours to the trip before one could finally fall asleep in the hotel. Today the air journey is only 13 hours and, with the introduction of rapid and very comfortable bullet trains to Nagaoka *(shinkansen)* the last leg of the journey can be made in only 3 hours from Narita.

On reflection it took me over 12 years and many visits to make any serious impressions to the Nishikigoi community who bred their stocks year in and year out in an area of the world that captivated me instantly and has continued to do so ever since.

The area I am writing about here is known as Yamakoshimura in Niigata Prefecture. This area of true outstanding beauty consists of around twenty small villages set high in the mountains where many of the most famous Nishikigoi breeders in the world have their homes. *(I suppose this area can be compared to the Yorkshire Dales or the Lake District although it is much smaller than either of these.)*

Yamakoshi is only a mere six miles distant from Nagaoka City which is a large, modern bustling place where one can find any creature comfort one desires in this very pleasant and hospitable city.

However, it may just as well be a thousand miles away!

For the first-time visitor, travelling for only 20 minutes from Nagaoka to Yamakoshi, the culture shock is significant.

The flat, wide and modern roads of Nagaoka and its shops and modern, concrete buildings soon give way to twisting, narrow roads climbing ever upwards. The modern brick houses are now replaced by ancient and traditional wooden homes wherein three generations of families dwell. There are rock escarpments, wild racing mountain streams and lush forests which produce incredible arrays of colours as autumn approaches every year.

Nestled within all of this beauty are the tiny villages themselves each bearing wonderful and strange names. It is, indeed an area of true mystique which I have since become to know far better than the geography of my own home town and surrounds.

The villagers themselves came from rice farming stock several decades ago and it is said that over 80% of these folk are involved in one way or another with producing Nishikigoi today.

I have covered all the other Nishikigoi areas in Japan on many occasions. Some of these areas indeed have their very own forms of outstanding beauty *(Mihara, in Hiroshima is one)* but Yamakoshi is where Koi were first 'invented' and, for me, Yamakoshi will always reflect the true spirit of these creatures.

Several 'non-Koi' guests have accompanied me here at times. They all, without exception, remark as to how breathtaking the area is and also how wonderful, friendly and hospitable the families are that they have met on their journeys throughout the Yamakoshi mountainsides and villages.

**The 'haunting mystique' that is Yamakoshimura**

I consider myself extremely fortunate, over many years, in both purchasing and selling, *in monetary value,* probably more Nishikigoi than any other person I know of outside of Japan.

This, in turn, has enabled me to return again and again to ask more questions of these special folk who have forgotten more of both Nishikigoi and their production than the rest of us can even begin to comprehend.

After my necessary and lengthy period of apprenticeship involved in visiting and re-visiting these breeders again and again, they gradually began to 'open up' to this inquisitive and dogged foreigner *(gaijin)* who seemingly would not go away. Soon they began to answer the multitude of questions that had been swirling around in my head for many years.

Since those very early days, these Nishikigoi breeders have been my mentors in just about everything to do with my chosen vocation in life. Just about all of the information I have given the reader elsewhere in this book originated from these very same people.

If I had to sum up all of their information in one single word it would merely be **'simplicity'**.

**The tiny Koi village of Mushigame showing all the Nishikigoi breeders therein**

Every time I see or hear of the many *'groundbreaking innovations'* advertised by many manufacturers around the world and also their promotional claims that their product today will *'revolutionise the hobby of Koi keeping in the future'*. I simply pause for thought and wonder why not one single 'innovation' has yet been adopted by any of my teachers who continue to produce their stocks which are improved upon with each passing year.

Surely, if the expensive advertising blurb is as stated, then the first to adopt these products would be the breeders themselves? Alas no, instead these guys just get on with the task of producing the very finest Nishikigoi in the world with their own experiences and those learned over many years from their local contemporaries.

**Keeping Nishikigoi will never, ever become a 'science' despite many who profess otherwise.**

These talented breeders produce their stocks by spawning their valuable parent stocks in June to produce fry. These fry are then fed daily and grown from June in outdoor mud ponds *(doro-ike)* throughout the very warm summer months right up to harvest time in early October.

After this, all of their stocks are taken into their indoor, heated Koi houses where they will remain until the following June safely away from the ravages of a Yamakoshi winter. This is no different to a rice farmer planting his rice in spring and harvesting it in autumn.

**The peaceful and ancient Fukushoji temple in Koguriyama village**

**'Koi in the Mud' – the pond has been part-drained and is now shallow enough to wade and harvest. We can now see the Koi through the murky waters.**

The number of Nishikigoi mud ponds throughout Yamakoshi is significant and, at first, is hard to take in. Just about every spare inch of suitable and available land has been carved out of the mountainsides by machine. It is said that the actual clay in the area has properties rich in essential minerals which helps to produce the incredible pigmentation and skin quality of the Koi after harvest. The properties of this clay surface is said to last for three or four seasons, after this all the empty pond surfaces are scraped away by machine to around 6" and then removed. After this, fresh new clay is added and compacted firmly by machine to ensure the entire pond remains watertight.

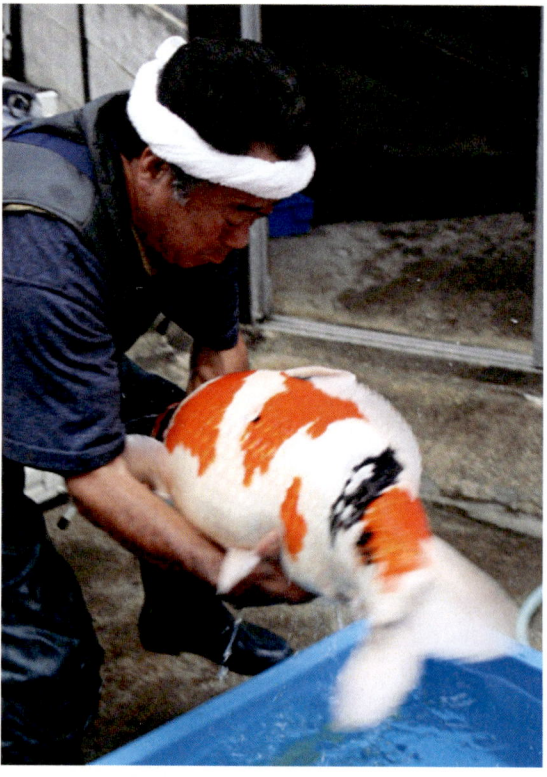

**Kazuto Ikarashi harvest – these Koi are being returned to his concrete ponds after harvest**

Today, there are some 400 or so Nishikigoi breeders throughout Yamakoshi and, over the years, I guess I have visited each and every one – some on countless occasions. Many have large outlets and are world famous whilst others are content to carry out their trade and remain happily in the background of the industry as 'unknowns'.

**Mud pond Nishikigoi harvest in Yamakoshi.**

This should give an idea as to the actual size of some of these ponds.

*Just imagine, in earlier days these were all excavated by hand!*

**The snow and ice can also prove to be a very real problem at times!**

Whether a breeder is big or small, important or unknown, they all know each other well and the respect between these individuals is great. From time to time they all buy or exchange stocks from each other and also assist each other free from charge at harvest time. It is still said that around 50% of the monetary value of worldwide Japanese Koi sales is retained within the Koi industry itself. This is by way of breeder buying from breeder; breeder selling to dealer; enthusiast selling to breeder etc. etc. Over 90% of these breeders trade from home and 'staff costs' are by way of their wives and sons.

The harvesting of the mud ponds takes place from early October to late November. It is during this period that the villages come alive with dozens of narrow wheel based trucks carrying zip-top containers and leaving give-away signs by water trails all along the narrow roads on the way, or on the way back, to and from the mud ponds. It is also at this time of the year when buyers from all around the world come to check out the harvests and purchase new stocks. During these months the sleepy mountain villages are transformed into hives of activity and very real excitement. This is the only real time of the year when vast numbers of Koi are sold.

**Left** – Hunting in October for larger sizes of Koi after the mud pond harvests.

**Right** – Koi hunting in April for smaller sizes after they have been fed and grown since October in indoor heated Koi houses.

**The Koi pictured above were photographed immediately after they had been harvested from the mud ponds. All these Koi were produced by Masaru Saito of the Shintaro Koi farm in Mushigame village**

The quality of body shape, skin lustre and pigmentation really begins to shine even more after they have spent around another three weeks in the indoor concrete ponds. In Sanke and Showa varieties the sumi (black) pigmentation increases significantly and begins to stabilise. All three Koi pictured above are tategoi of the highest order.

It is not possible to detail all my Japanese mentors in the space I have available but I feel I should highlight a few in no order of importance save to say that these guys and many others have played a significant part in the attempt of *'Educating Mr. Peter'*.

### Toshio Sakai

This man produced the 'Matsunosuke' bloodline of Sanke that are now famous with Koi enthusiasts everywhere. He improved on his late father's original line by introducing 'Magoi blood' to produce sizes unknown of before. He was raised and learned his trade in Mushigame village. Toshio now trades from Isawa in Yamanashi Prefecture.

So many superlatives have been documented about this man before and many of them written by myself. Toshio is the eternal 'challenger' who simply sets his sights on producing the very best Nishikigoi in the world today.

### Tsuyoshi Kawakami

His grandfather is famous in producing the original 'Torazo' *(Tiger)* Sanke which later played a significant part in the equally famous Jinbei line of Sanke.

Tsuyoshi's late father, Hiroshi introduced me to many Nishikigoi breeders during my early years. His farm is situated on the main street of Uragara village and is officially named as 'Urakawa' – but everyone simply knows it as 'Torazo'.

### Senichi Mano

Owner of **Izumiya Koi farm** in Iwamagi village, Izumiya is said to be the first-ever Nishikigoi outlet in the world.

They have always been famed throughout Japan in the sale of true 'jumbo' Koi and today produce the finest jumbo Yamabuki that can be found anywhere.

Senichi plays a major part today in the All-Japan Nishikigoi Dealer's Association *(Shin-Ko-Kai)*, he is also well known in the area for keeping fighting bulls.

Several famous breeders have also trained here notably 'Yagozen' and Manabu Ogata of the Ogata Koi farm.

On a recent visit to Senichi he greeted me by saying - in perfect English - *'Mr. Peter – the pioneer'!*

### Futoshi Mano

Owner of the world-famous **Dainichi Koi farm** in Minaminigoro village which was originally named after a shrine on his land.

His late father Minoru Mano first stabilised the bloodline of 'Dainichi Kohaku' around 1978 and then proceeded to produce true world-class Showa and Kohaku.

This is an extremely large outlet which has other houses for very special Koi near Ojiya City.

Several famous Koi breeders of today trained with Dainichi notably Marudo and Nogami.

### Masaru Saito

Owner of the **Shintaro Koi farm** in Mushigame village. He produces Go-Sanke varieties including wonderful Sanke from Isawa Matsunosuke lines.

Masaru has helped me greatly in obtaining details of the true history of Nishikigoi by obtaining permission for me to access the records kept in the Yamakoshi village office.

His father Shousuke started the farm in the late 1950's in the production of Yamatonishiki and other Hikarimoyo varieties.

### Mitsuo Hasegawa

Based in Ojiya City. His main production is Kohaku originally from Manzo and Tomoin bloodstock. Over the years I have bought many superb Koi from this outlet.

His knowledge in the keeping of water quality has to be so, in view of the high stocking rates he has.

I am proud to have first introduced his Koi to the UK in 1982.

### Daisuke (left) and Toshinori Ishihara

These young and very expert guys are based in Mushigame village at the **Yagenji Koi farm.**

This farm produces Go-Sanke plus Shiro Utsuri, Kikusui and some Kawarimono.

They always place great importance in displaying their stocks in sparkling clear water.

They are still under the watchful eye of their severe, but very jovial father, Yaichi.

### Seiji Hiroi

This outlet is based near Ojiya City and is named as **'Kokugyokan'** *(House of Champions)*.

He breeds very few Koi of his own but instead purchases tategoi from many high quality breeders throughout Yamakoshi and then develops them by his own techniques.

To be able to do this, one has to have a very acute 'eye'. Seiji proves this by supplying countless Supreme Champion Nishikigoi to many shows in all parts of Japan.

### Fujio Oomo

Fujio owns the **Oomo Koi farm** near Ojiya City. He is a relatively new breeder to the Yamakoshi scene but has been a Nishikigoi enthusiast for many years. His initial teachings came from the late Shoji Tanaka but today he learns much today from his neighbour Hisayaku Nogami.

He has a great advantage in speaking perfect English and has assisted many overseas visitors to the Yamakoshi area for several years now.

His farm is situated near to Ojiya City and he specialises in the production of Showa varieties which are now becoming well known by other breeders in the area.

**Typical winter scene in Yamakoshi superbly captured in oil**

**Mud pond in winter, Mushigame village**

**'Koinoburi' (Carp Streamers) - denoting strength and flown on 'Boy's Day' in May**

**Shrine in Yomogihira village**

The mighty **Shinano River** – Japan's longest. This was taken with Ojiya to the right and Nagaoka to the left. For many years now, the breeders in the surrounding mountainsides have discarded unwanted Koi into the streams running by their homes. All these streams discharge into the Shinano as it makes its way towards Niigata City and thence pours out into the sea. This river now contains many large Nishikigoi in most varieties and some enormous Magoi that can exceed 1.3 metres.

# Just where is Yamakoshi?

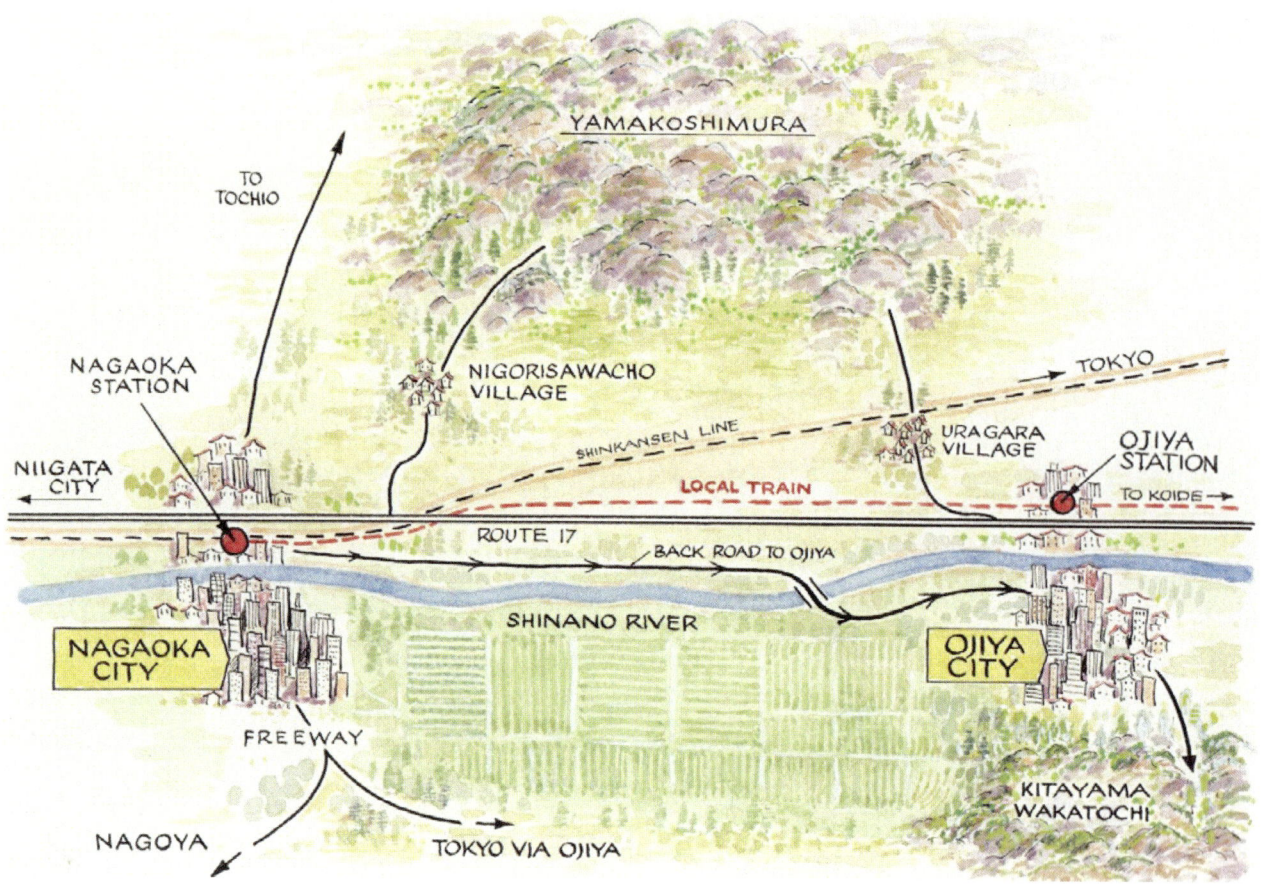

Simply, Yamakoshi is in Japan's Niigata prefecture some 200km north west of Tokyo City.

For visitors to Yamakoshi, there are two cities equally near to the area, one being Ojiya and the other is Nagaoka where very good, modern hotels and restaurants can be found. The Shinkansen *(bullet train)* from Tokyo station only stops at Nagaoka which means a further 20 minute ride on the local train is required to reach Ojiya.

The above unique painting has been specially prepared to give visitors, basing themselves in either choice of city, their bearings on arrival. Each city bridges the Shinano river. Also the main route 17 trunk road, together with the local rail line, passes through each city.

I have shown access roads to Yamakoshi from both cities. If one is staying in Nagaoka then the entrance to the area is via Nigorisawacho village along route 17 as shown. If one is staying in Ojiya then the entrance to the area is via Uragara village also along route 17.

The map shows directions to villages not in the Yamakoshi area such as Koide, Kitayama and Wakatochi plus directions to Tochio from where other villages such as Tashiro; Tanesuhara; Terano; Iketani; Okubo; Naranoki; Kogomo and Komatsugura can all readily be accessed. In all these outlying areas Nishikigoi can be found at smaller outlets. From time to time, I have located several excellent Koi from these villages.

Before I reluctantly close this final chapter, please enjoy the scenes below.

### Takezawa village scenes in springtime

The spring vegetation comes alive and the mud ponds have been filled with melted snow water. This is the 'quiet time' of the season before the breeding of the parent Koi commences.

This famous stone monument is sited in the very centre of Takezawa village and commemorates the true birthplace of Nishikigoi. A rare part of the world today that is in true peace with itself.

**If Nishikigoi are a part of your life, then you should really take time to witness the beauty that is Yamakoshi for yourself. I promise, you will not regret it!**

*'Well, that's just about all folks, yet another Koi book finally completed. I really do hope that it has been and will remain to be of value to you. Mountains of thanks to my wonderful wife Hilary who brought me endless cups of coffee and constant, unfailing encouragement - Stewart Jones - 'the street-wise kid'; 'the mysterious Garry HB' & Carys; Peter & Sheilagh Chester; Ian Stewardson; Sean Hunter; 'Man' & Wendy; Jasper Kuijper; Ken Wilkie; Stuart Parker; Alan Raw and many others – thank you all so much for just believing.'*

..................................................................................Waddy

Sayonara!